# Rio Grande
## In Color

## Volume 1: Colorado

## by Ross B. Grenard

Published by
**Morning Sun Books, Inc.**
11 Sussex Court
Edison, N.J. 08820
Library of Congress Catalog Card Number: 92-080547
Typesetting by R. J. Yanosey of Morning Sun Books.

First Printing
ISBN  1-878887-11-4

*Illustrations from D&RGW memorabilia -*
*- collections of Bob Yanosey and the author*

# Dedication

**To all those who remember the Rio Grande as it was during those years.**

**To those who worked for it at the time and are my friends.**

**To those who read these words and wish they might have been with us.**

**And most especially to those of the Rio Grande family whose memory is eternal in my mind, this volume is sincerely dedicated.**

*Ross B. Grenard, Lock Haven, Pa.*
*March, 1992*

# Foreword

In writing about the Rio Grande, it is virtually impossible to begin without acknowledging that group of individuals whose efforts during the long night of bankruptcy ensured that it would be operating in years to come. Their contribution was immense, both to the world of transportation and to those, who like myself have found it both a compelling and physically beautiful railroad to watch and to describe.

The idea for this book and the suggestion that we cover the epochal years we did, are those of Robert Yanosey, and he has my eternal gratitude for having suggested it to me. He has also been of great assistance in a number of other areas related to the work, and has suggested several ways to go about my task.

I am eternally grateful to those whose photographs are reproduced in this and the following volume. These include Bob Andrews, , the Don Ball Collection, David Barret, Jim Calvert, Mike Davis, Ed Fulcomer, Wes Haas, Ronald C. Hill, Vicktor Laszlow, Robert A. Le Massena, Chick Kerrigan, Roland P. Parsons and Lloyd Stagner. I would also express my appreciation for the assistance given me by Augie Mastrogiussepie in his position as Railroad and Photographic Specialist for the Western Collection of the Denver Public Library, in arranging for the use of the Otto Roach transparencies at the Rio Grande Collection there.

In writing of the Rio Grande I must acknowledge a debt of gratitude to the employees of that railroad who have over the years contributed to the sum of my knowledge on that specific subject. Especially must I acknowledge Jackson Thode, whose researches are invaluable to anyone wanting to know the how and why of the railroad during any period of its existence. A lifelong employee of the railroad whose honors include receiving the George Hilton Award from the R&LHS for bringing to light the work of company photographer George L. Beam, Jack is one of those whose view

of this period can be expressed as "... all of which I saw, part of which I was."

At the same time there were others, too numerous to mention, in all departments and locations who were happy to discuss their railroad and its activities over the years that it was so much a part of their lives. For their railroad was, in the last analysis, a complicated property, which can never be entirely separated from either its spirited history or its largely perpendicular geography. It contains a number of surprises for those encountering it for the first time, and even journeymen experts are not immune to discovering new aspects of its operations, past or present.

To those who have made their feelings manifest that the extensive bibliography of the Rio Grande is out of all proportion to its place in American railroading; I would counsel forbearance as it is the feeling of many that there remains still a story to be told, and hopefully not oversimplified. For if the Rio Grande is less than the "Holy Grail" of the railroad industry, it will do until something better comes along.

Lastly, anyone writing of the Rio Grande must be struck with the transitory nature of railroading as it has existed there. For even though most of the illustrations in these volumes were taken since Eastman Kodak began the enhancement of Kodachrome's speed from ASA 10, they would be impossible to duplicate today. For railroading is ever changing and even though most of its rituals endure, the participants do not.

Throughout its history, the area served by the Rio Grande has been one in which change is predominant. This element, and the many historical coincidences often give to the author a feeling that it is not entirely by chance that things are as they are. And one is left to ponder Canon Kingsley's words which are so much a part of Colorado's cultural heritage "So fleet the works of men back to the earth whence they came ancient and holy things fade like a dream."

# Introduction

The employees referred to it as the Río Grande, its management as the Rio Grande, and the financial community as "The Denver." But whatever one called it, they must admit that there were few like it historically, scenery-wise, or operationally. Particularly was this true during the seminal quarter-century when it transformed itself from a ward of the courts to a railroad whose physical plant, financial condition, and efficiency of operations were second to none in an industry which was then suffering an impressive lack of respectability.

Yet it was not always so, for often it seemed more involved with merely surviving than in attempting to become an operational benchmark. It had been ill-used by George Gould to finance the westward march of his transcontinental railroad system. For a time, not only its solvency but its ownership were in question. It was certainly no stranger to the reorganization process, and there have been in the past efforts to divide it up among connecting railroads seeking those parts most complimentary to their operations. That it continued to exist as an independent entity nearly into the 21st century, has been a testament to the abilities of its officers and employees, for not only did they have to operate a railroad under conditions beyond imagination through a largely perpendicular profile, but they had to do it competitively.

Small wonder then that Lucius Beebe referred to it as "the grandest mountain railroad of them all," or that John Barriger, when directing the Railroad Division of the Reconstruction Finance Corporation, described it as "the most difficult operating procedure seen." It has inspired both prose and poetry and attracted the finest in photographic talent to its many facets. In that sense it is somewhat larger than life, or has seemed so to many of its true believers throughout its corporate life. For even as the railroad of Beebe and Warman, and of "wooden cars and iron men," whose trackage had been constructed to such points as Ibex, Anthracite, Calumet, Floresta, and Silver Cliff was fading into the mists of history, a new railroad, no less heroic, was coming into place. It is this railroad we celebrate in this pages. Though it is gone as surely as the earlier eras it has left an imprint on those who witnessed and participated in the process, for one would have been extremely or totally emotionless not to have been impressed with what transpired.

Today (1992), this Rio Grande, whose independence had been such a cause celebre' for so many years is passing from the scene into one of the megasystems into which railroading has evolved. Rightly, not as the supplicant, but rather as the rock upon which the new contender is built. "Say neither it is blessed or cursed but only it is here" is what the poet said of an earlier period, and it is perhaps best to adopt a similar policy in this case. Yet if the mainline, standard gauge Rio Grande is to disappear into memory, it is well that we remember what it represented during an era when it stood forthrightly as an independent and innovative railroad, serving the public at all times, and was considered a force to be reckoned with by all it encountered.

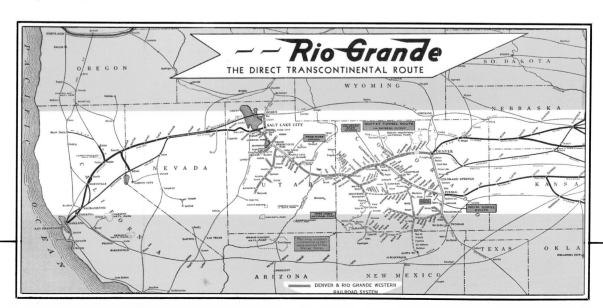

# Roster

Since the locomotives of the D&RGW during this period have been the subject of several formal rosters in publications, the following roster is of necessity sketchy and intended only as a quick reference for the reader, whose inquiries are referred to the Colorado Railroad Museum's publications. Also Joe Strapac's Rio Grande Diesels, Volumes I and II contain the story of the road's dieselization and the first and second generation diesels deployed to accomplish the feat. While none of these publications has been updated to the 1980s, they do constitute the most authoritative works thus far.

## STEAM

| Numbers | Wheel Arrangement | Builder | Notes |
|---|---|---|---|
| 58-62 | 0-6-0 | Baldwin | Out of Service by 1951 |
| 605, 634 | 2-8-0 | Baldwin | O/S by 1951 |
| 1002, 1024 | 2-8-0 | Baldwin | |
| 1031-1039 | 2-8-0 | Alco-Schdy. | ex-D&SL |
| 1132-1199 | 2-8-0 | Alco-Schdy. | |
| 773, 784 | 4-6-0 | Alco-Brooks | WP 94 built to same specs |
| 800-805 | 4-6-2 | Baldwin | |
| 1200-1213 | 2-8-2 | Baldwin | |
| 1220-1227 | 2-8-2 | Lima | ex-D&SL, only Limas on D&RGW |
| 1228-1229 | 2-8-2 | Alco-Schdy. | |
| 1400-1409 | 2-10-2 | Alco-Brooks | |
| 1501-1530 | 4-8-2 | Alco-Brooks | 1511-20 had boosters |
| 1600-1609 | 4-8-2 | Baldwin | 3 cylinder, world's heaviest 4-8-2 |
| 1700-1713 | 4-8-4 | Baldwin | |
| 1800-1804 | 4-8-4 | Baldwin | |
| 3300-3306 | 2-6-6-2 | Alco | |
| 3350-3351 | 2-6-6-2 | Alco | ex-N&W, acq. 1942 |
| 3400-3414 | 2-8-8-2 | Alco | compound Mallets |
| 3500-3509 | 2-8-8-2 | Alco | |
| 3550-3564 | 2-8-8-2 | Baldwin | ex-N&W Y2's |
| 3600-3619 | 2-8-8-2 | Alco-Brooks & Schdy. | Simple Articulateds. |
| 3700-3714 | 4-6-6-4 | Baldwin | |
| 3360-3375 | 2-6-6-0 | Alco-Schdy. | D&SL compounds |

## DIESELS, 1947-1972

| Numbers | Diesel Model | Builder | Notes |
|---|---|---|---|
| 38-43 | 44-tonner | GE | 1941-42 |
| 66-74 | VO660 | Baldwin | 1941 |
| 100 | NW2 | EMD | 1941 |
| 101-119 | S2 | Alco-GE | 1941-44 |
| 120-123 | H10-44 | FM | 1948 |
| 150-152 | H15-44 | FM | 1948 |
| 130-139 | SW1200 | EMD | 1964-65 |
| 140-149 | SW1000 | EMD | 1966-68 |
| 3001-3028 | GP30 | EMD | 1962-63 |
| 3029-3050 | GP35 | EMD | 1964-65 |
| 3051-3093 | GP40 | EMD | 1966-71 |
| 3094-3115 | GP40-2 | EMD | 1972 |
| 4001-4003 | ML-4000 | Krauss-Maffei | 1961 |
| 5100-5113 | GP7 | EMD | 1950-52 |
| 5200-5204 | RS3 | Alco-GE | 1951 |
| 5300-5304 | SD7 | EMD | 1953 |
| 5305-5314 | SD9 | EMD | 1953 |
| 5315-5340 | SD45 | EMD | 1967-68 |
| 5401-5424 | FT | EMD | 1942-three 4 unit sets |
| 5431-5474 | FT | EMD | 1943-five 4 unit sets |
| 5481-5514 | FT | EMD | 1944-first units eq. for psgr. svc |
| 5521-5544 | F3 | EMD | 1946 |
| 5561-5564 | F5 | EMD | 1948-one 4 unit set |
| 5551-5554, 5571-5644 | F7 | EMD | 1949-six 4 unit sets |
| 5651-5694 | F7 | EMD | first cab units del'd w/four digit #'s |
| 5701-5764 | F7 | EMD | 1952-six 4 unit & two 2 unit sets |
| 5762-5763 | F9B | EMD | 1955-to augment 1952 two unit sets |
| 5771-5774 | F9 | EMD | 1955-one 4 unit set |
| 5901-5924 | GP9 | EMD | Intended for ML frt svc in three 4 unit consists |
| 5931-5954 | GP9 | EMD | 1956-completed dieselization |
| 6001-6003, 6013, 6011 | PA1 | Alco-GE | 1947-two 3 unit sets for CZ |

Unlike a number of railroads, the renumbering of diesel units has never been a preoccupation with the Rio Grande. In fact, up to the recent Southern Pacific amalgamation, the only such major activity came in March of 1950, when the cab and B units received four digit numbers to simplify the dispatcher's task, avoid confusion in train orders, and was a recognition that they would operate independently as necessary.

# Denver Union Station

Since this volume is arranged as a tour of the Rio Grande's standard gauge lines, it is obvious that any such trip should commence at its headquarters city, and proceed south, since that was its pioneer trackage and thence west along the two mains which converge at Dotsero to funnel their traffic west along the Colorado River and across Utah to connections at Salt Lake and Ogden, where connections were made with the Western Pacific, Southern Pacific and Union Pacific Railroads. In addition to this, a number of branches add their carloadings to the main stream to be interchanged with other carriers at the four key junctions in Colorado and Utah. In years past, these included livestock, perishables, lumber, and non-ferrous ores. Of late, this tonnage has been almost entirely coal, of either metallurgical or steam quality, for domestic or import customers.

In the years illustrated, the Rio Grande was very much in the passenger business, and though the number of trains using the DUT had declined, it was still a major terminal during the quarter century herein described, and only after the near complete shift of passengers, mail and express to other means of transportation in the mid-Sixties did daily service vanish. (For a full history of the DUT from its founding in 1881 to the coming of Amtrak, see *Denver's Railroads*, published by the Colorado Railroad Museum in 1981, which pretty well covers the nuances of its corporate life.)

Of all the Rio Grande passenger trains to use the station, perhaps the most fascinating during these years were 9 and 10, the YAMPA VALLEY MAIL, as they appeared in their last reincarnation complete with the PAs for power, a regular two car consist and from 1962 to 1968, an annual last run during the winter season. Inherited from 1947 merger partner Denver and Salt Lake, it provided local service over

that erstwhile railroad's 231 miles to Craig through some of the finest scenery in Colorado. The Rio Grande's last strictly local service, it had commenced service behind 4-6-0s (out of a separate terminal because the owners of DUT had blackballed the Moffat Road from joining their club), and did not move in until 1947, when the Rio Grande absorbed the line. Discontinued at the end of 1950 in favor of an overnight train in conjunction with THE MOUNTAINEER, it was restored to service on Sept. 5, 1954 and operated until March of 1968.

At the other end of the spectrum were the seasonal Ski Trains operated on weekends from Christmas until early spring to haul devotees of the sport to the ski area (Winter Park) whose development had come about because of its proximity to the railroad at the West Portal of the Moffat Tunnel. These continue even today and are a monument to the long association between the sport and the railroad dating back to the introduction of skiing in Colorado. By 1964, skiing had grown so popular at Winter Park as to require 17 and 18 car consists protected by 5 and 6 unit lashups of F7s, steam generator cars capable of supplying warmth to these massive consists, and every coach that the car foreman and the Passenger Department could obtain. Frequently, their length exceeded the train sheds and required the use of equipment from the Burlington, Santa Fe, and Union Pacific to accommodate the crowds.

*(Below)* In this scene on a cloudy October day in 1961, Train 9 is shown leaving DUT jurisdiction to head west. One can only hope that the passengers on this Sunday morning will outnumber the crew on this classy little journey off the beaten path.

*(Ross B. Grenard)*

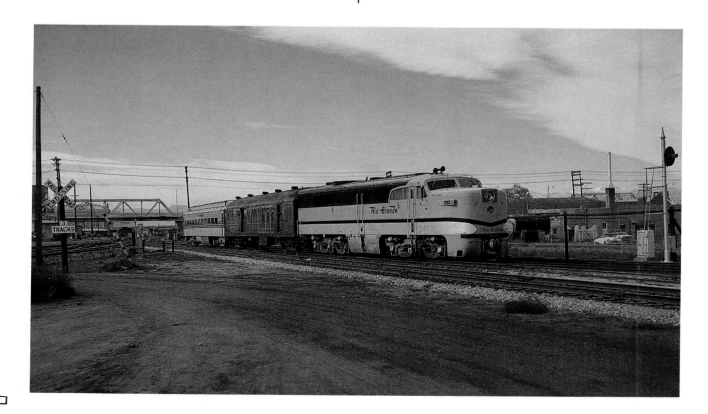

(*Above*) On a frosty March 28, 1964, Bob Andrews caught #5674 leading one of these 17 car consists under the 20th Street Viaduct and by the closed and soon-to-be-razed tower which once controlled all traffic through this end of the station.

(*Below*) In approaching twilight both for the train and a beautiful early September 1969 day, #5771 and four mates bring the "CZ" into town to wrap up the Rio Grande's responsibility on its eastbound journey that day. After the units are replaced by a trio of Burlington E's, #18 will back out of the station, pass through the rotating brushes on the wye at the Q's coach yard, and prepare to follow the high greens east towards dawn and Chicago. Even though the "Silver Lady" had become a bit disheveled and had but a short time to live, the participating railroads still maintained all of the rituals of service which revered it to its public.

(*Both- Robert W. Andrews*)

(*Above*) Even though the DUT had accepted the Moffat Road's trains in 1947, it somehow found a way, seemingly, to keep them out of the mainstream of morning activities as though it hoped to appease the spirits of the long gone railroad presidents who had kept them out in the first place. Consequently, the YAMPA VALLEY MAIL generally ended up on track 11, furthest from the terminal, and installed in the 1920s as an afterthought, to handle the electric cars of Colorado & Southern's Denver and Interurban subsidiary. Lacking an umbrella shed and many of the creature comforts of the other station tracks, it was a long and frigid walk for the passengers on such February mornings as this one in 1962 when #6013 awaited the highball.

(*Below*) Two years later, there was no argument as to who had track 1 nailed down as #5534 led a quartet of Fs ready to forward THE PROSPECTOR across the cordillera to Salt Lake City. Normally, two units were enough for the five car overnighter. So the reason for the additional power is open to conjecture. In any event #7's passengers should enjoy an on time performance, enhanced by the excellent dining service, aboard equipment acquired in 1950 when the C&O realized it had splurged excessively.

Once fondly and accurately described as "The Judge's Train," it was conceived by Wilson McCarthy to prove that his railroad could operate an overnight train from Denver to Salt Lake in competition with the Union Pacific. The first effort, featuring 2-unit Budd trainsets was less than successful for many reasons and it was perhaps as well World War II called an end to the experiment. Revived in 1946 #7 and 8 were a popular conveyance between the two cities and such intermediate points as Glenwood Springs, Grand Junction, and Provo.

(*Above - Wesley L. Haas, below - Robert W. Andrews*)

*(Bottom)* A few tracks out, a year earlier in August 1963, and just after 3:00 PM, #5484 has just arrived with the first section of #2 from Colorado Springs flaunting green flags and with an all-CB&Q consist soon to be incorporated into the consist of the DENVER ZEPHYR. The dome-coach, slumbercoach, and 10-6 sleeper operated between Chicago and "The Springs" and were carried on the ROYAL GORGE both ways south of Denver. Since the two trains connected perfectly at Denver, it was an ideal arrangement. Well, most of the time! Delays in either direction, missed connections, high water west of Pueblo, which resulted in #2's equipment being unable to get through, or freight derailments could result in additional sections being operated to protect the schedule and to assure that the Colorado Springs cars were properly incorporated into the nation's newest overnight stainless steel passenger train. In such instances, the Burlington paid the operating cost of the extra section and the power was whatever boiler-equipped units Burnham had on hand. The green flags are in compliance with Santa Fe operating rules, since that railroad had jurisdiction over all northbound movements on the Joint Line.

#5484 is one of the 1944 order of FTs delivered with 70 MPH gearing and boilers in the B units for passenger service. It was first operated on the EXPOSITION FLYER as #548, and was later split into two 2 unit sets as regular power on the postwar PROSPECTOR. Painted silver and black early in the game, the 548-84 remained in passenger service even after the rest of the FTs had their boilers removed and were regeared for helper service. By this date, the end of the FT era was in sight, and in March 1964, the entire set will be traded in on GP35s.

*(Wesley L. Haas)*

(Above) The Denver Union Terminal was content to let the proprietary railroads handle all passenger switching and as a result train-watchers were treated to considerable variety in yard power. Baldwin VOs seemed to be the Rio Grande's locomotive of choice for passenger switching duty during the years prior to their retirement. In June 1961, just two months short of its 20th birthday, one takes some spot time near the north throat after a busy morning of shuffling cars.

(Below) Just six years later, the railroad's sole NW-2 has the duty on a quiet July 4th. Generally a freight switcher, "Burnham's Pampered Pet" has just two years to go in Rio Grande service. In 1968, the 1941 La Grange product will be sold to Precision Engineering, which will in turn sell it to Great Lakes Steel.
(Above - Wesley J. Haas, below - Robert W. Andrews)

(Above)  For nine years after their arrival from LaGrange in 1946, the three F3 sets were prime passenger power between Denver and Salt Lake City.  After the demotion of the Alco PAs, they became standard power on the CALIFORNIA ZEPHYR, and remained so until their trade in late in 1965.  At Denver Union Station on a sunny August 2, 1961, #5524 awaits the air test prior to whistling off but not before showing off its striking new one stripe paint job to a father and his young son stepping forward to observe the matched 6,000 horsepower consist which will soon forward them and the 11 car consist.  In a few minutes, the blue flag will come down and all will be in readiness for another luxurious journey *Thru the Rockies, Not Around Them.*

(Below)  Five years later in 1966, both the Denver Union Terminal and Fairbanks-Morse H10-44 had seen their best years, as the 1000 horse switcher took some spot time in the near-deserted station after performing its work during the morning rush hour.  The years ahead will see the attrition of the station until under Amtrak, only five of the passenger tracks are needed, and #122 will, in January 1968, be sold to Precision Engineering as scrap, only to be re-sold to the Frisco who will discover it to be in such fine shape as to make it operable for the next two years. The 122's sisters will not be so fortunate.  Two of the class will go in trade to EMD on SD45s, and the last-con-structed #123 will be scrapped by Precision for parts.

*(Above - Don Ball Collection, below - James B. Calvert)*

# Denver Terminal

The Denver Union Terminal's trackage ended on the north at 21st. St., and on the south at the trestle over Cherry Creek. It was odd by reason of having an apex in the approximate center, which was due to the construction of passenger and baggage subways. Since its elevation was less than a mile high (5188 feet) the station and the surrounding area of yards, industrial trackage, and mainlines into DUT were often at the mercy of the South Platte and its tributary Cherry Creek, when flash floods occurred.

Nevertheless, during the years depicted, the area was honeycombed with trackage for interchanges and to serve various warehouses, industries, and power plants. Most of this has since vanished and, for instance, it is impossible to get out of the station and head south. Most of these yards are no longer active, and in one case Denver's major league baseball stadium is to be constructed on the sight of a former yard. Even before the 1980s, the freight houses, team tracks, and gantry cranes once so much a part of railroading were

totally redundant. In this area, the produce terminal once so prized by the Rio Grande is now the site of a community college.

This spot, the Wazee Market, by reason of its proximity to downtown Denver was a popular place for the Rio Grande to display its new hardware, the "CZ" for example, or for celebrations such as the one in May 1952 for the premiere of *Denver and Rio Grande,* a cinematic version of "The Royal Gorge War." For the occasion, 2-8-0 #268 was brought from Gunnison for a reunion with the Hollywood luminaries it had upstaged during its filming and exhibited next to freight diesel, #5401-04 (the railroad's first). The ceremony featured Rio Grande officials, the principals of the production, politicians, and the military.

*(Above)* For the occasion, a third rail was laid down by the local section gang, and the Burnham hostling crew managed to keep the 1882 Baldwin steamed up for a couple days. After which, it was back to work for all and sundry including the locomotives. This was the second such sabbatical for #268, normally concerned with hauling of coal and cattle on branch lines.

*(Left)* In a scene a little more typical of recent terminal operations, SW1000 #144 returns from the Cherokee Plant of Public Service of Colorado to North Yard with a long string of empty hoppers for forwarding back to the mines. Delivered only a few months earlier, the SW1000s still have their footboards and have not as yet been fitted with spark arresters. The gritty scene shows a little of the industrial activity present on the Northwestern Terminal's Belt Line.

*(Above - Ross B. Grenard, below - Wesley L. Haas)*

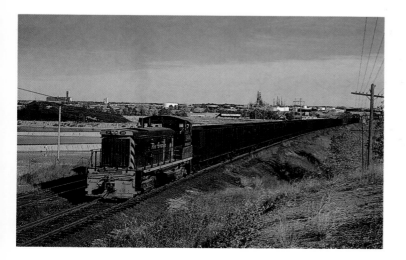

(Above)  While the trackage rights situation within the Denver Terminal was nowhere near as complicated as those prevailing in Chicago, Kansas City, St. Paul or other major rail centers it could, at times, be quite confusing to the uninitiated.  Here is one example in October 1964 as THE ROCKY MOUNTAIN ROCKET on its way to Denver Union Terminal for a noon departure passes a Union Pacific RS1 on Rio Grande trackage a mile or so south of the terminal. The explanation is simple for THE ROCKET has just been turned and serviced at Burnham, while the ex-Spokane International Alco is picking up an interchange cut from the Rio Grande's 7th Street Yard. Rock Island E8 #648 has come in for some kit-bashing along the way, for neither its fire engine red paint scheme nor its number boards seem standard either for the Rock or for E8s. Today, this scene is totally changed, for THE ROCKET is long gone, the RS1s were traded to EMD on the short-lived "Centennials," the Rock Island is but a fragrant memory, and even this trackage soon may succumb to urban renewal and rising real estate prices in the renovated and regentrified Arauria area of the city.

(Right)  A year later at the same spot, F5 #5561 leads a football special south for the Air Force Academy-Notre Dame confrontation at Falcon Stadium.  The 1948-built EMD and its 17 car consist are just passing the southern limits of Denver Union Terminal trackage (the searchlight signal just parallel to the first coach) and will operate over the D&RGW's Denver Subdivision to South Denver interlocking where the Joint Line commences.  The stadium at the Academy was adjacent to the southbound line and for several years until train-offs caused the railroad to retire or sell off much of its passenger equipment, Rio Grande football specials were a popular way for Denverites to travel to and from the games on fall Saturdays.

(Both - Ross B. Grenard)

In snowy November 1961, PA 6013 and PB 6012 lead the ROYAL GORGE past the same spot on its trip to Grand Junction where its through cars will be incorporated into the consist of the Denver-Salt Lake PROSPECTOR which will leave some 8 1/2 hours later and operate via the Dotsero Cutoff and Moffat Tunnel. The GORGE trains carried to the end of their days numbers one and two, dating from the days when they were the railroad's premier passenger trains and a journey from Denver to Salt Lake featured open top sightseer cars through the Royal Gorge, and a sidetrip covering Marshall Pass and the Black Canon of the Gunnison were high on any visitor's list. While it appears that a mountain winter has begun early and in earnest, don't bet on it for a week later this snow will have melted and those couch potatoes now reclining in front of their TV sets will be out golfing and cycling.

*(Ross Grenard)*

**THE ROYAL GORGE**

For 70 years America's Best-Loved Travel Wonder, the awesome Grand Canyon of the Arkansas River is now more popular than ever with transcontinental travelers. Vista-Dome cars, now part of the regular consist of the Royal Gorge trains, give travelers a new appreciation of the beauties of this historic route.

MAIN LINE Rio Grande THRU THE ROCKIES

DENVER AND RIO GRANDE WESTERN RAILROAD
THE DIRECT CENTRAL TRANSCONTINENTAL ROUTE
Printed in U.S.A.

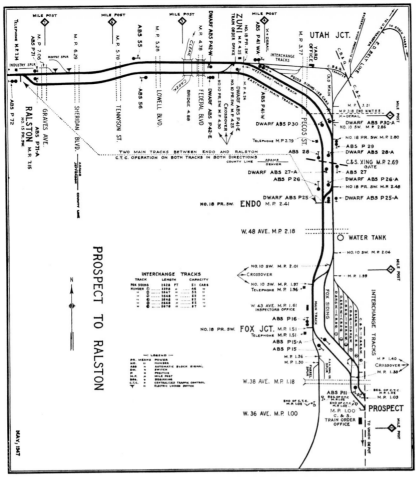

Denver Terminal area prior to completion of North Yard on
September 1, 1949

Special passenger trains of all sorts were a feature of Rio Grande operations until the late 1960s, and one of their busiest summers was to occur in 1960, as within two months both a national Shrine convention and the International Boy Scout Jamboree were held in Denver and near Colorado Springs respectively. All the railroads serving the area had their share of special trains, and a number of groups chose to supplement the convention by returning over the Royal Gorge and Moffat Tunnel Routes, and consequently that time was a great one for passenger miles operated. In another scene from the Denver Terminal area, soon to be famous F9 #5771 leads four units on their last lap into Denver with a band of nobles whose special was received off the Missouri Pacific at Pueblo, and whose itinerary included spending the morning at Colorado Springs.
*(Ross B. Grenard)*

# The Associated RRs of Colorado

In a Christmas card setting, "Burnham's Pampered Pet" heads home from the Denver Federal Center with a lone empty box car over trackage which once carried the Denver-Golden interurbans of the Denver Tramway. Largely remembered as the operator of an extensive 3'6" system, the Tramway used its standard-gauge trackage for both suburban service and freight operation. In 1942, a branch was constructed to serve a small arms plant then under construction by the Federal Government at Remaco (named for its operator Remington Arms) southwest of Denver. Since the flow of freight soon inundated the two electric locomotives and one crew of Tramway subsidiary Denver and Intermountain, the Rio Grande agreed to provide supplementary service on what was presumed to be a "hostilities-only" basis.

After the war, the government-owned facility became the Denver Federal Center and still houses the Western Regional offices of many agencies. It also serves as a major distribution center for the General Services Administration, supplying government agencies in the western US. Consequently, freight business remained quite good. In the meantime, the Tramway abandoned passenger service on the line in 1950, and freight service three years later. Consequently, a consortium consisting of the Rio Grande, Burlington, Colorado and Southern, Rock Island, and Santa Fe, styled as the Associated Railroads of Colorado purchased the trackage and operated it until 1989 when the trackage was sold to the Denver Rapid Transit District. In practice, the trackage was operated for themselves and the others by the Rio Grande and the Burlington Northern (as corporate successor to the C&S) on a rotating basis. Prior to the abandonment of electric service in 1953, the 100 and the other switchers which might be assigned to this trackage were equipped with dummy trolley poles to activate the crossing signals on suburban streets.

*(Wesley L. Haas)*

| AUTOMATIC BLOCK SIGNALS | | |
|---|---|---|
| | 1.0 | |
| CX | PROSPECT | DNJP |
| | 0.5 | |
| | FOX JCT. | P |
| | 0.9 | |
| | ENDO | P |
| | 1.5 | |
| | ZUNI | P |
| | 2.9 | |
| | RALSTON | P |
| | 5.3 | |
| | LEYDEN | P |
| | 5.6 | |
| | ARENA | P |
| | 3.2 | |
| | CLAY | P |
| | 3.3 | |
| | PLAIN | P |
| | 6.8 | |
| | CRESCENT | P |
| | 5.7 | |
| | CLIFF | PW |
| | 4.7 | |
| R | ROLLINS | DP |
| | 5.2 | |
| | TOLLAND | P |
| | 3.2 | |
| | EAST PORTAL | PY |
| | 6.8 | |
| RV | WINTER PARK | DNP |
| | 5.3 | |
| Z | FRASER | DP |
| | 3.8 | |
| RN | TABERNASH | DBFKP SWY |
| | 9.8 | |
| B | GRANBY | DP |
| | 10.4 | |
| GS NS | SULPHUR | DFKSP YW |
| | 6.8 | |
| | FLAT | P |
| | 5.0 | |
| | TROUBLESOME | P |
| | 5.5 | |
| X | KREMMLING | DNPW |
| | 2.3 | |
| | GORE | P |
| | 5.5 | |
| | AZURE | P |
| | 5.1 | |
| | RADIUM | P |
| | 6.6 | |
| | YARMONY | P |
| | 5.8 | |
| OD | ORESTOD | DNJPW |
| | 5.6 | |
| | McCOY | P |
| | 4.3 | |
| | CRATER | PY |
| | 4.0 | |
| | VOLCANO | P |
| | 7.4 | |
| | EGERIA | PW |
| | 3.2 | |
| | TOPONAS | PY |
| | 4.6 | |
| | TRAPPER | |
| | 3.9 | |
| WA | YAMPA | DPW |
| | 6.2 | |
| BG | PHIPPSBURG | DNBFKO PSWY |
| | (168.0) | |

Two Main Tracks

Schedule Time
Average Miles per Hour

# Prospect (Denver Terminal)

*(Right)* The PAs were still getting calls to handle #17 and 18 in the summer of 1958, when #6011 and company passed Prospect and entered CTC Territory 1.10 miles from the Denver Union Terminal. As the stainless steel consist glides past the Burlington red Train Order office, a Colorado and Southern 2-8-0 pauses on the lead from Rice Yard before heading out to switch along its mainline north. The C&S (now Burlington Northern) paralleled the Rio Grande's main as far as Utah Junction, before diverging to go their separate ways. The C&S line to Golden since 1949 operated over Rio Grande trackage rights to a point some two miles west of Denver. A manual interlocking, Prospect saw trains of many types and railroads during its years as an open office: C&S narrow gauge trains to Silver Plume, Denver and Interurban electric cars, and all sorts of steam and diesel power operated by the Burlington Lines and Rio Grande in both passenger and freight service.

*(Below)* After encountering home trackage for the first time on this July 29, 1964 morning, #5521 leads the CALIFORNIA ZEPHYR past Fox Junction and on towards points west. Since leaving Union Station, it has operated over DUT, and Colorado & Southern trackage, and now is technically on that of the Northwestern Terminal which owned the line from Prospect to Utah Junction. Leased by the Grande in 1947, as corporate successor of the Denver and Salt Lake, the NWT was a vital link between Denver's terminal and the trackage rights obtained in 1934 to operate thru the Moffat Tunnel. The Rock Island's freight cutoff to North Yard, constructed in 1951, also used a part of the NWT to link up to expedite connections. Having figured in a number of disputes, this Nevada Corporation was finally acquired by the railroad and absorbed in 1969, but not after a squabble with the minority stockholders was resolved.

Now largely bereft of activity, Fox Junction was the interchange point for transcontinental traffic with the Burlington Route after the opening of the Dotsero Cutoff in 1934. It was abandoned after the opening of North Yard in 1949. Prior to that, Moffat Tunnel freights originated in Burnham, picked up their Rock Island and Denver-originated traffic at 7th Street, transited the Union Station, picked up the "Q" blocks here, and then headed west in an operation hardly conducive to competition with the UP. Consequently, the terminal consolidation which began with North Yard was, in fact, the beginning of a competitive service.

*(Above - David Barret Collection, below - Robert W. Andrews)*

# Burnham

The Rio Grande's principal shop facility was located along what was then its mainline, southeast of Denver. Named for George Burnham, one of the principals in the Baldwin Locomotive Works, it came into being to repair the minuscule cars and locomotives of General Palmer's "Baby Railroad." Its functions expanded with the railroad and came to include a massive locomotive and car shop, headquarters of the Mechanical Department, roundhouse, coach yard, and research lab. During its history, it has constructed, rebuilt, upgraded, and maintained virtually all types of railway equipment of both narrow and standard gauge persuasion. A shop worthy of a railroad several times the Rio Grande's size, its craftsmen have at various times produced open platform observation cars, narrow gauge 2-8-2s, some of the first insulated box cars in railroading, and returned to service a million pound 2-8-8-2 which had previously been cut into three pieces to retrieve it from the Colorado River. While priding itself on its craftsmanship in all areas, Burnham was above all a locomotive shop.

Trained to steam, but not wedded to it, it early became a diesel shop of excellent reputation and performed such precision tasks as grinding crankshafts with the same consummate skill it applied to setting valves, rolling flues, or modifying cutoffs. The history of Burnham and its accomplishments has yet to be written, but it should be. For without its skill and muscle, the Rio Grande would never have become the railroad it was.

*(Opposite page)* On a sunny July day in 1961, three F7A units sun themselves at the 36 stall Burnham roundhouse while awaiting assignment. None of the trio have as yet received the MU nose plugs so noticeable in later pictures, and are still running in A-B-B-A formation with, perhaps a GP9 spliced in between for service on manifests in response to the horsepower race on Chicago-West Coast freight which has produced elephantine consists of SD24s, GP20s, and DL-600Bs on Santa Fe, UP, and Cotton Belt manifests. Within a year, the F7s will be joined by KMs and GP30s as Stout Street fashions its response to the second-generation power in service on its competitors. Burnham performed not only classified repairs on all Rio Grande standard gauge power, but was the Denver base for inspections, running repairs, and oil changes on the diesel fleet. Since most freight and yard power was dispatched from North Yard at the other end of town, motive power transfers kept the hostlers busy at times as they moved incredible consists back and forth like pieces on a chess board. Interestingly, the EMDs here pictured are, in the long run, fated for extinction as surely as any of the steam locomotives which once occupied this spot, for the 5661 has only a little over two years left before it will be demolished on Soldier Summit and traded in on a GP35. The fates will be kinder to #5671 which will last until 1972 before returning to La Grange for reincarnation as a GP40-2, and, perhaps luckiest of all, #5664 will be sold, in 1970, to the Alaska Railway for a new life as its #1532.

The largest steam locomotives to frequent Burnham in the last years of steam were the L131 and L132 class 2-8-8-2s, twenty of which were constructed by Alco in 1927 and 30. Weighing in at roughly 1,000,000 lbs. and exerting 131,800 pounds tractive effort they were used in freight and helper service out of Denver and remained the largest intact class of standard gauge steam until 1955. After 1952, they were used principally during the fall rush seasons on Denver-Pueblo freights and in helper service between Tabernash and the west portal of the Moffat Tunnel. It was in this latter service that they ran their final miles in 1956.

*(Below)* Two years earlier on a bright September morning, #3605 awaited the highball for points south. While such service might have seemed a comedown after a life spent battling the grades of Soldier Summit and Tennessee Pass, the 1927 Brooks alumni will have its work cut out for it on the 1.42% grades between Louviers and the 7,237 foot summit at Palmer Lake. Soon the air test will be complete, the conductor will hand up the orders, and Extra 3605 will be off over the railroad's pioneer trackage trailing a cloud of smoke which would terrify the ecologists of a later generation, and create envy in the heart of any destroyer officer ever charged with laying down a smoke screen.

*(Opposite page - Ronald C. Hill, below - Robert Le Massena, Grenard Collection)*

# Visitors

The engine terminal at Burnham supplied locomotives to protect any and all assignments out of Denver, and in addition to its owner's power handled Rock Island and Missouri Pacific passenger units. Prior to 1951, it serviced the former road's freight engines, chiefly 4-8-4s and Mikes when they laid over in the Mile High City. These required the staff to become versed in the idiosyncracies of oil-burning steam locomotives, an unknown quantity on a railroad whose own steam power burned some of the finest locomotive coal in the West.

*(Above)* However, the E-units used by both lines were relatively trouble free and required only turning and fueling before returning east. The MP did occasionally send Alco PAs west, but most of the time EMD products got the call. As here in early 1963, E7 #20, in the Downing Jenks economy blue scheme awaits its afternoon call to head THE EAGLE close by the sign identifying the area as belonging to "Colorado's Home Railroad."

*(Left)* One of the most widely-traveled units to visit Denver in the 1960s was Missouri Pacific #42, nee Boston and Maine #2133, that railroad's only E8. Easily spotted by its headlight, differing in appearance from that of others of its class, and by its buzzsaw decal rather than the eagle used on other MP passenger units, it was acquired after the B&M dropped its last conventional passenger trains, dipped in blue, and became the last of all passenger power placed in service on the far flung *Route of the Eagles.*
*(Both - Ross Grenard)*

# Krauss-Maffei

While short-lived and never duplicated, the Krauss-Maffei units ordered in association with the Southern Pacific cut a handsome figure during their short tenure at Burnham. In fact, they became star boarders there since nearly every trip over the line seemed to bring them back for modifications to make them more compatible with the railroad's demanding requirements, unyielding profile and harsh environment. Since a litany of their operating problems is beyond the scope of this text, suffice to say that their import to the Rio Grande made a great deal of sense at the time they were ordered but that they never lived up to their potential. They did sound an alarm bell at La Grange concerning second-generation dieselization, and pointed up some of the failings then inherent in a follow-the-leader motive power policy. And in that sense perhaps, they were successful.

*(Above)* #4002, here shown sunning itself beside the long unused coal chute, was delivered in November of 1961 after an eventful trip form Houston. Constructed in Munich the summer before, it still looks very much as built. Improved air intakes and electrical MU connections to replace the air throttle are still in the future, but for the present the three 4000 horsepower "Messerschmidts" are the railroad's hope for years to come.

*(Below)* A month earlier, in January 1962, sister unit #4003 was modified with side air ducts to allow its twin Maybach diesels to obtain enough pure air while passing through the numerous tunnels on the line. Since #4003 nearly always occupied the trailing position in power consists, this was a necessity for successful operation. Later, these chimneys will be removed and replaced with air grills on the lower carbody which would suck in pure air not as yet contaminated by the exhausts of the lead units. These chimneys neither improved the esthetics nor enhanced the clearance diagrams of the three. *(Both - Wesley L. Haas)*

# EMD Hoods

*(Opposite page, top)* In September of 1968, the SD45s used in pool service on the Kaiser Steel coal trains were repainted to show a large GRANDE on the hood and while #5331 was not one of the assigned units, Burnham did repaint it in the new scheme after one year's service. Here it sits, in June of 1969, outside the shop to show that black and orange can arrest the eye when it is fresh. Eventually the new lettering became standard for all the second-generation power delivered, and older hood units were lettered in the new scheme as they received shoppings. With the exception of the passenger units, such repaintings always seemed a low priority item and some units seemed never to be treated to such extravagance.

*(Opposite page, bottom)* Such would seem to be the case with the first six-axle unit, SD7 #5300, here shown outside the new shop building at Burnham. Still in an early tiger stripe, it shows no signs of cosmetic attention since delivery in 1953. Since these locomotives rarely appeared on mainline freights, and for the most part toiled on coal mine branches in Utah and Colorado where tractive effort was more important than appearance, this was to be expected.

*(Above)* The 5101 was the doyen of all road-switchers to go into service. Delivered in October, 1950 it served in both branch and road service until 1972, when most of the serviceable GP7s were sold to the power-short Rock Island in an arrangement where an equal number of RI derelict Fs were traded to EMD on D&RGW GP40-2s. The arrangement seemed to satisfy both railroads, and the power, then old enough to vote, was rebuilt by Morrison-Knudsen and served that ill-starred carrier to the end of its days. In 1962, though, #5101 was very much the property of the D&RGW and had just been painted in a scheme matching the GP30s. Here it sits at the south end of Burnham awaiting the return of the crew from lunch.

*(Opposite page, top - Wesley L. Haas, opposite page, both - James B. Calvert, above - Ross B. Grenard)*

# Adjusted Tonnage Ratings And Car Limits

| FROM | TO | Class F-9 GP-9 577 5901-5954 | Class FT-F-7 540-547 549-551 555-576 | Class F-3 552-554 | Class SD-7-9 5300-5314 | Class GP-7 RS-3 5100-5113 5200-5204 | Adjustment Factor |
|------|----|----|----|----|----|----|----|
| | | Tons | Tons | Tons | Tons | Tons | Tons |
| Denver | East Portal | 920 | 850 | 630 | 1350 | 800 | 3 |
| Tabernash | Winter Park | 950 | 890 | 675 | 1400 | 885 | 4 |
| Orestod | Tabernash | 1760 | 1630 | 1235 | 2600 | 1655 | 6 |
| Orestod | Toponas | 920 | 850 | 630 | 1350 | 800 | 3 |
| Phippsburg | Toponas | 1190 | 1100 | 750 | 1550 | 1200 | 4 |
| Phippsburg | Pallas | 1760 | 1625 | 1250 | 2600 | 1900 | 6 |
| Haybro | Phippsburg | 1190 | 1100 | 750 | 1550 | 1200 | 4 |
| Steamboat | Haybro | 1700 | 1575 | 1200 | 2600 | 1900 | 6 |
| Craig | Steamboat | 3400 | 3150 | 2400 | 4300 | 3550 | 9 |
| Pueblo | Portland | 3500 | 3350 | | 4000 | 3350 | 9 |
| Portland | Canon City | 3350 | 3200 | | 3800 | 3200 | 6 |
| Canon City | Salida | 1500 | 1390 | 1060 | 2000 | 1390 | 4 |
| Salida | Tennessee Pass | 1325 | 1225 | 900 | 1900 | 1200 | 4 |
| **Minturn | Tennessee Pass | 595 | 550 | 390 | 900 | 512 | 2 |
| Grand Jct. | Glenwood | 2025 | 1875 | 1500 | 3100 | 1800 | 6 |
| Glenwood | Minturn | 1400 | 1300 | 975 | 2050 | 1250 | 6 |
| Glenwood | Bond | 1500 | 1400 | 1100 | 2150 | 1400 | 6 |
| Glenwood | Leon | 1700 | 1650 | | | 1650 | 2 |
| Leon | Aspen | 850 | 800 | | | 800 | 2 |
| Malta | Eilers | 700 | 650 | | | 650 | 2 |
| Eilers | Leadville | 600 | 550 | | | 550 | 2 |
| Salida | Maysville | 800 | 750 | | 1100 | 750 | 2 |
| Maysville | Monarch | 380 | 340 | | 530 | 340 | 1 |

*(Opposite page, top)* GP7 #5100 was delivered in 1950 as #5104, and was renumbered in June of 1951. Here it appeared in August 1962, still wearing its first tiger stripes. Although quite striking originally, this paint scheme seemed prone to show the scars of mountain railroading.

*(Opposite page, bottom)* Fated to be the final Alco locomotive purchased by the Rio Grande, #5204 was acquired in June 1951, as the last of an order for five RS3s. Intended to run long hood forward as opposed to the Geeps delivered the year before, they were delivered without numbers on the side of their cabs, and with steam type classification lamps. Originally assigned to Denver-Phippsburg coal trains and to the Joint Line, they were victims of unintentional over-scheduling, based on the idea that road-switchers could function as on a 24 hour utilization cycle. Perfect in theory, it proved less so in practice. In any event, the five RS3's ended up in switching and transfer service at Denver and Pueblo, where they remained until acquired by Precision Engineering for scrap in April 1966. Regular power around Denver, #5204 was the only RS3 repainted in the switcher paint scheme.

*(Below)* Crankcase explosions were generally unheard of after the lab at Burnham began a program of spectrographically analyzing diesel lube oil samples for fuel leaks and foreign matter. The program also served to indicate whether the oil required changing or not, so was a plus on both counts. One such explosion did occur to B unit #5423 in February 1962, and it was considered reason enough to retire the unit then and there, dispatching it back to La Grange on the first GP30 trade. Here it is shown ready at the Burlington interchange for its last journey. In contrast, several of the other four unit sets were in such excellent shape that they operated under their own power back to La Grange - somewhat like walking to one's own funeral.

*(Opposite page, both - Wesley L. Haas, below - Ross B. Grenard)*

In 1952, the steam power which had been deployed on the Salt Lake Division was brought east to operate out of Denver and Pueblo. The decision to sell off the Salt Lake City Shop was a motivation, as were the anti-smoke ordinances passed there since the 1940s. At any rate steam on the mainline was becoming very rare by then, and only a few seasons remained, largely during the fall rush. Already, eight of the fifteen 4-6-6-4s had been scrapped, victims of the influx of F7s and the nickel steel boiler shells used on the 1938 order. The latter malady was one which plagued numerous classes of modern locomotives built in the late 1930s, and was a fault peculiar to no single locomotive class, type and builder.

(Above) #3710 was constructed by Baldwin in 1941, first in an order of five, which were to be the last built to the railroad's own specifications. They weighed 1,035,330 pounds ready for service, and developed 105,000 pounds of tractive effort. Larger than the Union Pacific's 3950s. they were exceeded in weight only by the NP and SP&S engines of the same wheel arrangement. The fifteen shared with WM 1401-12 the distinction of being Baldwin's only "Challenger" types. Retired in 1955, #3710's career had encompassed both the most prestigious and least romantic service imaginable. Used originally on fast freight across the Utah Desert, the locomotives of its class had functioned equally well on heavy passenger trains during World War II and after, lugged coal over Soldier Summit, and ore trains from Salida to Pueblo. Even reduced from center stage to bit parts they were impressive. So it was on an early fall morning in 1952, as it leaves Burnham for Pueblo, embodying all that was memorable about the articulated era on the Rio Grande.

(Above - Robert A. Le Massena)

*(Right)* Burnham saw its first standard-gauge steam locomotives in 1881, when the Denver and Rio Grande began operation of mixed gauge trains between there and Pueblo and dispatched its last just three quarters of a century later. The last active steam there was number 1163, a 2-8-0 constructed by Schenectady at a time when the Rio Grande had come under the sway of George Gould, who envisioned it and its Pacific Coast extension, the Western Pacific, as integral parts of his transcontinental railroad system. It, and the sister engines of class C-48 had long outlived that tragic era, survived some three bankruptcies since, and served the railroad in both primary and ancillary capacities wherever its standard gauge track led. Now, on a sunny November 10, 1956 afternoon, #1163 has its fire cleaned for the last time hard by the lab building where electron microscopes are analyzing diesel oil, and even now all manner of researchers are pondering what the future motive power requirements will be. Was it perhaps significant, symbolic, or merely coincidental that the two eras should meet thus?

*(Left)* As the evening shadows begin to fall in June 1969, #5338 and two B units head out of town just south of Burnham Yard. Since the SD45 is one of those normally assigned to Kaiser pool service with the UP, and even fitted with the latter road's cab signals and train radio, one may speculate on what it is doing in Denver. As for the "Odd Couple" power lash up, we can only guess. But in any case 7600 horsepower should give the tonnage a ride. The engineer appears enthusiastic, in part because of the higher pay rate on the 389,724 pound behemoths, and partly because it might expedite the train to Pueblo and get the consist interchanged before midnight, thus saving his employer 24 hours per diem on foreign cars and the crew a long trip.

*(Above - Ross B. Grenard, below - Wesley L. Haas)*

## THE DENVER  & RIO GRANDE

# North Yard

Opened for traffic in 1949, and intended to expedite transcontinental freight on the Moffat Tunnel Route, North Yard quickly became the major terminal in Denver and resulted in the consolidation of several smaller yards and the elimination of the D&SL's Utah Junction facility. Two years after it opened, the Rock Island constructed a freight line linking the Union Pacific Kansas Division trackage rights over which they reached Denver with the Northwestern Terminal Belt Line to begin operating into the facility, with their diesels laying over there between runs. Consequently it was a busy place as proved in Ron Hill's March 1979 overview *(opposite page, top)* of the servicing tracks. The arrival and departure tracks, Rio Grande Motorway intermodal terminal, and Cargill Corporation's grain elevator are in the background.

*(Opposite page, bottom)* Prior to the Rock Island's demise, their locomotives were regular customers and such scenes as GP40 #4716 (whose purchase was financed incidentally by the Union Pacific) and host road's #5322 together were daily occurrences.

*(Above)* Over the years, General Electric sent out several sets of demonstrators in an attempt to break up the seemingly monogamous relationship between the Rio Grande and EMD. The first arrived in April of 1962, and involved a three way test between the GP30's, the KMs and high hood U25Bs. Here the three GEs, whose logo leaves little doubt as to their owner, and the dynamometer car are preparing to couple up and head west.

*(Opposite page, top - Ronald C. Hill, opposite page, bottom-GP40 - Roland P. Parsons, above- Wesley L. Haas)*

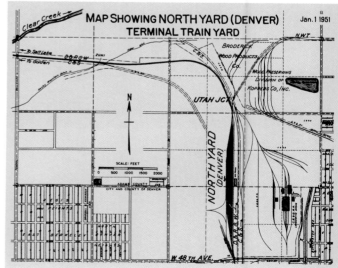

*(Opposite page, both)* The initial "No Sale" did not deter GE from attempting to break up the relationship and, in 1967, seeking to capitalize on the problems western railroads had been having with the GP35 electrical systems, sent the U33Bs west for a stint. On September 2, 1967, #301 heads a four unit consist and the dynamometer car, as they are readied for a westbound and receive considerable attention from a crowd gathered around the third unit.

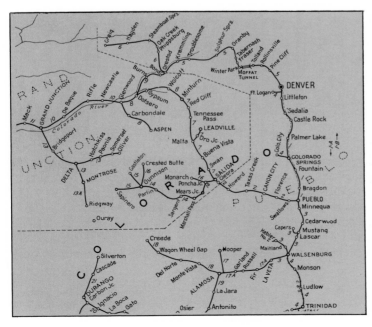

*(Above)* In a scene a little more prosaic, a newly repainted #5944 and a mixture of F7s and regeared FTs bring in the overnight PMX from Phippsburg. The symbol stands for "Moffat Extra" carrying Public Service of Colorado coal. While there had always been coal business off the Craig Branch, it had yet to expand into the traffic boom of the seventies which would bring SD40-T2s, unit coal movements, CTC, and welded rail to the one time Moffat Road. The thrice-weekly and often daily PMXs carried merchandise, cattle, and lumber in addition to the individual cars of coal. #5944 is just passing the crossover switch at Utah Jct., where the Rock Island and Northwestern Terminal's Belt Line to the stockyards diverge from the Rio Grande main.

*(Opposite page, both - Ronald C. Hill, Grenard Collection, above - Ross B. Grenard)*

*(Below)* Switching duties at North Yard were largely handled by the ubiquitous Alcos S2s until their replacement by SW1200s in the mid-60s. During those years, the sounds of North Yard were heaven to Alcophiles as the 112, shown here in September 1961 awaiting word from the yardmaster as to its next assignment, and its brethren kicked cuts of cars or struggled upgrade with transfer drags from yards in the Platte bottoms.

ALCO

*(Opposite page, both)* Just at twilight on a warm September evening, the south end of the yard basks in a moment of quiet, while 5110 and 113 relax before again commencing work. Soon the activity will escalate as the "A" blocks begin rolling down South Boulder Canyon, the teletypes begin to spew out consists and yarding instructions, and "all concerned" begin their tasks to ensure that foreign cars and expedited shipments get interchanged to the Burlington by the "witching hour" of midnight to save a day's per diem. The Rio Grande found out early that lesson #1 in becoming a profitable bridge carrier is to cut down on car hire, and getting cars interchanged to connecting lines within 24 hours is one way to do it. This changed in the 1970s when ICC Per Diem Rules were modified, but until then it made for fascinating operations.
*(All - Wesley L. Haas)*

# Short, Fast Freight

In 1965, in conjunction with a motive power pool that saw Rio Grande GP30s and 35s operating into Chicago, Chinese red Burlington second-generation units began handling run-through freight to Salt Lake. While such operations were not new to the CB&Q, it was the first time Rio Grande freight units began showing up regularly on connecting railroads. The new train, symbolled "CX" was preblocked at Clyde Yard and made no setouts or pick ups enroute to SP and WP connections. Its schedule from North Yard to Salt Lake equalled that of the CALIFORNIA ZEPHYR and it was intended as the centerpiece of what became a policy of "short, fast, frequent" manifest freights operating between its eastern and western connections, and hopefully expanding its share of forwarder, autoparts, and other high-rated commodities to West Coast destinations. Eastbound, the pooled units handled a new train "ASPD" which departed Ogden and Roper in the early hours of the morning and arrived in Denver for 8:00 PM delivery to the "Q."

*(Below)* Here, CB&Q #946 leads a quartet of Chinese red and grey units through North Yard enroute to adjacent 38th St. Yard and their home rails. It is a cloudy May afternoon, with the hint of an approaching spring storm, as the Rio Grande has, once again made the schedule. Besides the home team's SW1200s awaiting the arrival of their second trick crews, one can notice at the right of the picture a Sperry Rail Detector Car laying over.

*(Opposite page, top)* After the retirement of the S2s, yard and transfer work was assumed by the SW1200s received in early 1965, and the ten SW1000s which came from EMD between 1966 and 68. Their delivery and the use of GPs and SDs in more demanding yard assignments had allowed the retirement over three years of all first generation yard power. In July of 1965, a trio of the new locomotives seem to have the situation very much in hand as they stand in front of the terminal building.

*(Opposite page, bottom)* The first of the SW1200s, #130 was sent to Grand Junction to relieve the 1500 horse FMs on the hump, and to work with "slug" #25. The arrangement was less than satisfactory, and was abandoned in 1972. In this December 1970 scene, #130 having arrived from the western slope awaits a trip to Burnham Shops for a touch of paint, among other things.

*(This page - Ross B. Grenard, opposite page, top - Roland P. Parsons, opposite page bottom - James B. Calvert)*

(*Above*) During the period in which they were assigned to Denver-Salt Lake freights, the KMs regularly showed up at North Yard for minor service and fueling. Here, #4001 operating without the company of the other two units is readied for what must be some sort of test run. The date is early 1962, and we can assume that the configuration has to do with the GE-GM-KM tests then being undertaken. The Grande's GP30s were being set up about this time, and it is to be assumed that they will soon be on the scene. In the background can be seen the main terminal building with its airport-like control tower and yard office, the first to be erected at a Rio Grande yard.

(*Opposite page, top*) Before leaving the area, we should perhaps take a look back at the Denver and Salt Lake when Utah Junction was more than a set of weed-grown storage tracks dominated by a water tank whose peeling paint still declares it to be the property of the D&SL. Here, in a 1947 scene, 2-8-0 #123 and the railroad's transfer caboose are shown with the shops in the background. The D&SL had already been absorbed into the larger company for eight months, but it was still business as usual for the Moffat Road. Within a year, #123 and its contemporaries will be renumbered and lettered with the flying Rio Grande and in March 1951, the 1910 Alco which once knew the altitudes of Rollins Pass, will be retired.

(*Opposite page, bottom*) In March of 1964, fifteen years after Utah Junction had made up its last freight train, #3009 led the PCM west past the water tank on the first part of its journey. As the whine of the turbochargers and the "8th notch" exhausts echo in the chilly air it would seem they are telling the past that the torch long carried by the men and Mallets of old has been passed to a new generation.

(*Above - Roland P. Parsons, opposite page, top - Ross B. Grenard, opposite page, both - Wesley L. Haas*)

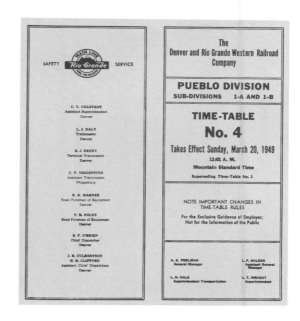

SAFETY — Rio Grande — SERVICE

The Denver and Rio Grande Western Railroad Company

**PUEBLO DIVISION**
SUB-DIVISIONS   1-A AND 1-B

**TIME-TABLE**

## No. 4

Takes Effect Sunday, March 20, 1949
12:01 A. M.
Mountain Standard Time
Superseding Time-Table No. 3

NOTE IMPORTANT CHANGES IN TIME-TABLE RULES

For the Exclusive Guidance of Employes; Not for the Information of the Public

C. V. COLSTADT
Assistant Superintendent
Denver

L. J. DALY
Trainmaster
Denver

R. J. HENRY
Terminal Trainmaster
Denver

C. F. NEIGENFIND
Assistant Trainmaster
Phippsburg

R. R. HARNER
Road Foreman of Equipment
Denver

P. R. FOLEY
Road Foreman of Equipment
Denver

S. F. O'BRIEN
Chief Dispatcher
Denver

J. B. CULBERTSON
H. M. CLIFFORD
Assistant Chief Dispatchers
Denver

A. E. PERLMAN
General Manager

L. F. WILSON
Assistant General Manager

L. H. HALE
Superintendent Transportation

L. T. WRIGHT
Superintendent

# The Joint Line

The Joint line was the creation of the USRA when it operated the railroads during World War I. In order to help eliminate congestion it combined the parallel lines of the Santa Fe and Rio Grande into a paired track arrangement. Since the two crossed over each other several times between South Denver and Bragdon, trains in either direction ran over the rails of both lines, (as is illustrated in the map). In order to minimize conflicts, the Rio Grande dispatched all southbound trains and the Santa Fe those bound north, with crews required to be qualified on both road's operating rules.

*(Above)* The Krauss-Maffeis were no strangers to the Joint Line, and here they are shown at South Denver, heading up a Pueblo-bound freight, early in their careers. In this perspective, one can see the pattern of the trackwork and in the foreground, the connection from the northbound line to the Santa Fe's line into Denver proper. It was regular procedure for Burnham to break in freshly shopped power on the line south, rather than risk the problems inherent with having it break down on the Moffat Line. The KMs were broken in between Burnham and Pueblo for several weeks before their ceremonial "maiden run" to Salt Lake.

*(Opposite page, top)* Just leaving Littleton, returning to Denver from Louviers, the 5943 rolls through South Denver suburbia on May 15, 1967.

*(Opposite page, bottom)* Late in October 1964, the 5534 crosses Dry Creek with the ROYAL GORGE. Only a couple of months remained for Train #2 as a through train.

*(Above - Ronald P. Parsons, opposite page, top - James Calvert, opposite page, bottom - Ross B. Grenard)*

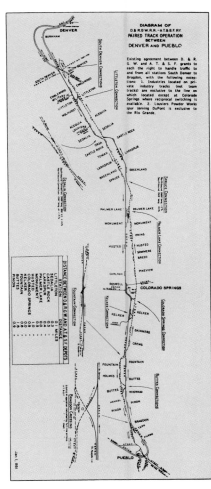

# Douglas County

*(Opposite page, top)* On the occasion of its last run, July 27, 1967, the southbound ROYAL GORGE receives a final salute from the operator at Louviers, not merely for the 5764 and its six car train, but for a long line of Train #1's which stretched back to the early days of the Rio Grande and whose pullman green consists had been the medium through which many Americans had discovered the scenic wonders of their country. Once it had hosted pullmans en route from the midwest to the Golden Gate, and its wide-windowed diners had boasted "Mountain Trout Fresh Every Day." Now it was ending forever: "The canons filled with smoke and the sound of gliding pullmans," the train butchers selling their books of tinted views along its rails, the ten minute pause for sightseeing in the spot where to quote the railroad "Man most closely approaches the infinite." But look again, for the railroad's last-delivered F7 is immaculate, and its consist the same. For even as the bean counters rejoice over its demise, the rest of the railroad has chosen to send off #1 on its last journey as befits a "train of tradition."

*(Opposite page, bottom)* Over the years since 1950, a number of different diesel models were used on the "Short" local, and on October 5, 1968, SW1000 #145 was doing the honors as it rolled home to Denver on Santa Fe trackage. Crossover were located at Littleton, Sedalia, Palmer Lake, Colorado Springs, and Fountain to enable trains to switch trackage for use as necessary. With the exception of Colorado Springs, there was very little local business on the line other than the Denver suburbs and the Dupont explosives plant. Consequently, such pick ups and setouts as were necessary were handled by through freights. Delivered just two years previous, #145 has been used mostly around the Denver area, and it would seem most unusual to use it on a local such as this when there were SW1200s active. However, the EMDs were geared for 50 mph, and could operated in place of their larger brethren when necessary.

*(Below)* Castle Rock, which looms above the town named for it and much of the Plum Creek Valley, is perhaps the dominant physical landmark between Denver and the summit. It now looks down on a community which has become a part of metropolitan Denver, but here it looks majestically on the passage of Extra 5644 north and 42 cars, principally empty Union Pacific ore cars. At this time, CF&I's blast furnaces were still active at the Minnequa Works, and were using hematite mined in Wyoming and Utah. This ore came in over the Rio Grande, Union Pacific, and Colorado & Southern, as the steel company tended to split up its freight business on the basis of rail purchases.
*(All- Robert W. Andrews)*

MOUNTAIN TROUT EVERY DAY IN THE DINING CAR

September the 3rd 1954, found #3615 resolutely plodding south on a freight for Pueblo. By that time, steam had largely disappeared from the Joint Line and the articulateds were active only in rush season (ie. peach season). 1954 was the next to last year for these great engines in Denver-Pueblo service.

(Robert A. Le Massena)

*(Above)* On a cold January 11, 1970 a quartet of C&S hood units led by a Burlington U30B rolls smokily south on a trainload of Coors Beer for the palates of thirsty Texans. The Adolph Coors Brewery was a major shipper on the C&S and the symbiotic relationship between the two has become legendary.

*(Below)* By 1972, Burlington Northern had become a reality and though the Colorado & Southern still existed in corporate form, it was for all practical purposes a division of the larger carrier. A rather dirty-looking F45 leads C&S freight #78 south near Greenland in the March 1972.

*(Both - Ronald C. Hill, Grenard Collection)*

# Palmer Lake

Palmer Lake is the summit of the line between Denver and Pueblo. Its elevation is 7237 feet and constitutes the divide between the Arkansas and South Platte Rivers.

*(Above)* On July 30, 1960 the Boy Scout Jamboree at Colorado Springs was ending and the railroads were engaged in transporting the youngsters home. The Rio Grande operated up to five sections of southbound #1 and several passenger extras. This is First #1 picking up orders at Palmer Lake as it rolls an impressive train over the summit.

*(Opposite page)* On December 12, 1962, an unusually heavy #1 headed around what one Rio Grande expert has chosen to describe as "Grenard's Curve." The train size that day would appear to be occasioned by Christmas season mail, and by several extra coaches chartered by a school organization off on a lark to Colorado Springs. In the background here may be seen something of the Palmer Lake community, and off to the right the lake itself. Three decades have come and gone since this picture was taken. Today Palmer Lake is no longer a sleepy little town but a bustling bedroom community for both Denver and Colorado Springs, #1 and the 6003 are long gone, the northbound line has been torn up from Colorado Springs to Palmer Lake, and what was then the southbound line has been equipped with CTC for bi-directional movement. "So," indeed, "fleet the works of men."

*(Both - Ross B. Grenard)*

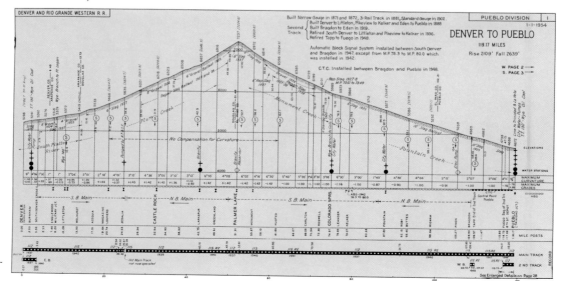

## EQUIPMENT
### No. 1—The Royal Gorge
+*Observation-Lounge Car:*
+*Standard Sleepers:*
Kansas City to San Francisco (153) 10 Sec. 1 DR. 2 Compt., via MP 15-D&RGW 1-WP 1.
Denver to Ogden (D-22) 10 Sec. 1 DR. 2 Compt.
+*Chair Car:*
Denver to Ogden.
+*Diner* (Service a la carte and table d'hote).

### No. 3—The Colorado Eagle
(Streamlined-Diesel Power)
+*Diner-Lounge* (Service a la carte and table d'hote).
+*Standard Sleepers:*
Denver to St. Louis (31) (32) (2 cars) 4 Dbl. Bedrooms, 14 Roomettes, via D&RGW 3-MP 12.
Denver to Wichita (34) 8 Sec. 1 DR. 3 Dbl. Bedrooms, via D&RGW 3-MP 12-412.
+*Planetarium Chair Car:*
+*Chair Car:*
Denver to St. Louis, via D&RGW 3-MP 12.

### Train No. 15
+*Standard Sleeper*—Denver to Alamosa (14) 12 Sec. 1 DR.
+*Chair Car*—Denver to Alamosa.
*Coaches*—Alamosa-Durango-Silverton. (See Table No. 4)

### Train No. 11
+*Coach*—Marysvale to Salt Lake City.

+ Air Conditioned.

## EQUIPMENT
### No. 2—The Royal Gorge
+*Observation-Lounge Car:*
+*Standard Sleepers:*
San Francisco to Kansas City (W-21) 10 Sec. 1 DR. 2 Compt., via WP 2-D&RGW 2-MP 16.
Ogden to Denver (D-10) 10 Sec. 1 DR. 2 Compt.
+*Chair Car:*
Ogden to Denver.
+*Diner* (Service a la carte and table d'hote).

### No. 4—The Colorado Eagle
(Streamlined-Diesel Power)
+*Diner-Lounge* (Service a la carte and table d'hote).
+*Standard Sleepers:*
St. Louis to Denver (111) (112) (2 cars) 4 Dbl. Bedrooms, 14 Roomettes, via MP 11-D&RGW 4.
Wichita to Denver (114) 8 Sec. 1 DR. 3 Dbl. Bedrooms, via MP 411-11-D&RGW 4.
+*Planetarium Chair Car:*
+*Chair Car:*
St. Louis to Denver, via MP 11-D&RGW 4.

### Train No. 16
+*Standard Sleeper*—Alamosa to Denver (14) 12 Sec. 1 DR.
+*Chair Car*—Alamosa to Denver.
*Coaches*—Silverton-Durango-Alamosa. (See Table No. 4)

### Train No. 12
+*Coach*—Salt Lake City to Marysvale.

+ Air Conditioned.

*(Opposite page, top)* After the completion of Falcon Stadium adjacent to its track at the Air Force Academy, the Rio Grande operated a large number of football specials. These carried passengers from Denver to football games in an atmosphere without traffic jams or pre-game congestion. On the way back these trains operated against the current of traffic from Academy siding to Palmer Lake where they crossed over to the northbound main. On October 17, 1964 with a rainbow in the background a group of faithful head home on a fall evening.

*(Opposite page, bottom)* On a summer morning in 1960, a second section of #1 heads south with the DENVER ZEPHYR connection for Colorado Springs.

*(Above)* At milepost 52, just south of the Palmer Lake station, #5641 rolls a short 18 car freight, mostly empty auto racks for the Missouri Pacific to hustle back to the Chevy plant in Kansas City. Included in its consist, though are two of the insulated "cookie boxes" used by Keebler to haul baked goods to its distribution centers. It is a lovely afternoon in May of 1966 as the two units prepare to round the lake and drop down the grade into the Monument Valley.

*(Opposite page, top and above- Robert W. Andrews, opposite page, bottom - Ross B. Grenard)*

# Flash Floods

*(Opposite page, top)* In the construction of their trackage over Palmer Lake Summit, both the Santa Fe and Denver and Rio Grande engineering corps chose to locate considerable trackage along the watercourse which can sometimes create problems in an area where a stream may be a trickle at best 99% of the time, but subject to flash flooding on rare occasions. This necessitated protecting rights-of way with rip-rap in potential areas of high water, a task engaged in on February 28, 1959 by #5924, a clamshell, and a work train. Since the alignment of the Rio Grande closely followed Monument Creek almost from its source to its confluence with the Fountain River south of Colorado Springs, flash flooding was always a threat to both the mainline and terminal facilities in "the Springs," and on occasion cloudbursts around Palmer Lake would send torrents of water careening downstream to disrupt matters. The buildings in the background are among the earliest completed at what would soon be the US Air Force Academy, where classes were already in session.

*(Opposite page, bottom)* To the south of Colorado Springs, the tracks to Pueblo and the mountains front range diverge to southeast and southwest, respectfully, with the railroad lines following the Fountain River to its confluence with the Arkansas at Pueblo, through an area more midwestern in appearance and hospitable to agriculture. Even so, it is an area of flash flooding, high water detectors for bridges, and where cloudbursts have disgorged torrents of water to wash away track, trestles, and on one occasion a complete train and its passengers. Rolling north through the soft light of a late August evening, #5574 has an eighteen car Colorado State Fair special heading home through such country just north of Fountain, Colorado. The six F7s are wide open in the 8th notch as they make a run for the 1% grade which begins just north of here at Crews and continues up the Monument Valley almost to Palmer Lake, where it stiffens to 1.42% for the last six miles.

*(Above)* The other partner in the Joint Line was John Santa Fe, whose freight and passenger trains utilized the operation. Here is one of their dual-service F7's on a southbound freight near Spruce.

*(Opposite page, top - Vicktor Laszlow, opposite page, both - Robert W. Andrews, above - Ross Grenard)*

# Colorado Springs

Founded, like the Rio Grande, by William Jackson Palmer, who allegedly disapproved of the conduct of the inhabitants of Colorado City, a community whose roots went back to the Pikes Peak Gold Rush, Colorado Springs was never a major industrial center as was Pueblo, or a mining town per se. General Palmer intended it as a center for the refined resident, vacationer, or health seeker. At one time during his residency there, it was such a popular place for English aristocrats, that it was referred to as "Little London." At one time it featured its own stock exchange and Palmer's Antlers Hotel rivalled any watering hole on the Continent. What industry there was, remained of the low profile type which did not generate great qualities of carloadings. Perhaps the closest it came to being a western boom town was during the years when it became the jumping off place for the riches of the Cripple Creek District. Located at the base of Pikes Peak and with the healing waters of the Manitou Springs close at hand, it began attracting tourists and sightseers from its earliest days, and has not stopped yet. Whether it was a desire to golf at the Broadmoor's manicured course, to ride a burro or a cog train up Pikes Peak, take the waters, or just relax, Americans came there and millions of them did it by train.

*(Below)* As would befit such an area, both the Rio Grande and Santa Fe depots were equipped with private car facilities, and since during "The Glided Age" Colorado Springs was a place entrepreneurs retired to after making their millions, we can assume that they were heavily patronized. By the 1950s, however, most visitors used the not unimpressive services of regular trains, such as the ROYAL GORGE here shown at the Rio Grande station as the morning's mail from Denver is off-loaded, and a young Alcophile looks on. Since #1 connected with most of the morning trains into Denver, it always did a considerable business southbound.
*(Don Ball Collection)*

**ST. LOUIS - KANSAS CITY - WICHITA - PUEBLO - DENVER**
**SALT LAKE CITY - SAN FRANCISCO**

OGDEN · SALT LAKE CITY · PROVO · DENVER · COLO. SPGS · KANSAS CITY · ST LOUIS · GRAND JUNCTION · GLENWOOD · SALIDA · CANON CITY · PUEBLO · WICHITA · OAKLAND · SAN FRANCISCO

**ROYAL GORGE ROUTE**
**MISSOURI PACIFIC — RIO GRANDE — WESTERN PACIFIC**

| READ DOWN | | | READ UP | |
|---|---|---|---|---|
| The Colorado Eagle | The Royal Gorge | SEE PAGE 3 FOR EQUIPMENT | The Royal Gorge | The Colorado Eagle |
| No. 11 | No. 15 | Missouri Pacific Lines | No. 16 | No. 12 |
| | | (Central Standard Time) | | |
| * 4 00 PM | * 1 50 PM | Lv St. Louis, Mo. ... Ar | *M 5 40 PM | *12 01 PM |
| 6 05" | 4 10" | Lv Jefferson City, Mo. ... Lv | M 3 20" | 9 45 AM |
| 9 00" | 7 45" | Ar Kansas City, Mo. ... Lv | M 12 20 PM | 7 01" |
| 9 10" | 8 30" | Lv Kansas City, Mo. ... Lv | 8 10 AM | 6 40" |
| 10 13" | 10 25" | Lv Osawatomie, Kan. ... Lv | 6 20" | 5 22" |
| :10 38" | 10 53" | Lv Ottawa, Kan. ... Lv | 5 23" | 4 53" |
| | 11 41" | Lv Osage City, Kan. ... Lv | 4 36" | 4 15" |
| 11 48 PM | 12 31 AM | Lv Council Grove, Kan. ... Lv | 3 46" | 3 38" |
| 12 14 AM | 1 03" | Lv Herington, Kan. ... Lv | 3 00" | 3 07" |
| | 1 42" | Lv Gypsum, Kan. ... Lv | 2 23" | |
| | 2 20" | Lv Salina, Kan. ... Lv | 1 45" | |
| | | | | |
| 9 30 AM | 9 30 PM | Lv Wichita, Kan. ... Ar | 7 00 AM | 7 00 AM |
| | | | | |
| 1 32 AM | 3 45 AM | Lv Geneseo, Kan. ... Lv | 12 30 AM | 1 51 AM |
| 2 07" | 4 45" | Ar Hoisington, Kan. ... Lv | 11 40 PM | 1 12" |
| | | (Mountain Standard Time) | | |
| 1 15 AM | 4 07 AM | Lv Hoisington, Kan. ... Ar | 10 24 PM | 12 02 AM |
| :4 46" | 9 11" | Lv Eads, Colo. ... Lv | 6 00" | 8 31 PM |
| :5 35" | 10 15" | Lv Sugar City, Colo. ... Lv | | ‡7 41" |
| 5 43" | 10 25" | Lv Ordway, Colo. ... Lv | 4 45 PM | 7 35" |
| 6 45" | 11 35" | Ar Pueblo, Colo. ... Lv | 3 50" | 6 50" |

| No. 4 | No. 2 | | No. 1 | No. 3 |
|---|---|---|---|---|
| | | (See table 1 for detailed schedules) | | |
| * 6 55 AM | * 3 30 AM | Lv Pueblo, Colo. ... Ar | *11 45 AM | * 6 40 PM |
| 7 45" | 4 35" | Lv Colorado Springs, Colo. ... Lv | 10 47" | 5 50" |
| 9 25" | 6 30" | Ar Denver, Colo. ... Lv | 8 50" | 4 10" |

| No. 1 | | Denver & Rio Grande Western | | No. 2 |
|---|---|---|---|---|
| | * 8 50 AM | Lv Denver, Colo. ... Ar | 6 30 PM | |
| | 10 47" | Lv Colorado Springs, Colo. ... Lv | 4 35" | |
| | 11 45" | Ar Pueblo, Colo. ... Lv | 3 30" | |
| | | | | |
| | 12 05 PM | Lv Pueblo, Colo. ... Ar | 3 10 PM | |
| | 1 28" | Ar Royal Gorge, Colo. ... Lv | 1 56" | |
| | 1 38" | Lv Royal Gorge, Colo. ... Lv | 1 46" | |
| | 8 15" | Lv Glenwood Springs, Colo. ... Lv | 7 30 AM | |
| | 10 50" | Lv Grand Junction, Colo. ... Lv | 6 00" | |
| | 6 23 AM | Lv Provo, Utah ... Lv | 9 51 PM | |
| | 7 30" | Ar Salt Lake City, Utah ... Lv | 8 50" | |
| | | | | |
| | 9 35 AM | Ar Ogden, Utah ... Lv | 7 10 PM | |

| No. 1 | | Western Pacific | | No. 2 |
|---|---|---|---|---|
| | | (Mountain Standard Time) | | |
| | * 8 30 AM | Lv Salt Lake City, Utah ... Ar | 7 45 PM | |
| | | (Pacific Standard Time) | | |
| | 10 00 AM | Lv Wendover, Utah ... Lv | 4 15 PM | |
| | 1 30 PM | Lv Elko, Nev. ... Lv | 1 10" | |
| | 4 10" | Lv Winnemucca, Nev. ... Lv | 10 35 AM | |
| | 6 10" | Lv Gerlach, Nev. ... Lv | 8 35" | |
| | 9 30" | Lv Portola, Calif. ... Lv | 5 45" | |
| | | (Feather River Canon) | | |
| | 1 55 AM | Lv Oroville, Calif. ... Lv | 12 35 AM | |
| | 2 33" | Lv Marysville, Calif. ... Lv | 11 40 PM | |
| | 3 30" | Lv Sacramento, Calif. ... Lv | 10 40" | |
| | 4 50" | Ar Stockton, Calif. ... Lv | 9 15" | |
| | 7 20" | Ar Oakland, Calif. ... Lv | 6 45" | |
| | | (3rd & Washington Sts.) | | |
| | 7 35 AM | Ar Oakland Pier, Calif. ... Lv | 6 30 PM | |
| | 8 20" | Ar San Francisco, Calif. ... Lv | 6 00" | |

\* Daily.
‡ Stops to receive or discharge revenue passengers.
M Missouri River Eagle.

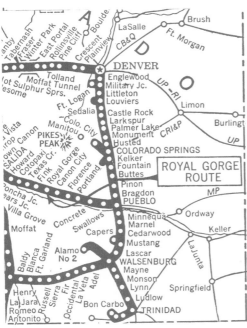

A year after the picture was taken, switch crews began adding and subtracting the through cars from the DENVER ZEPHYR and here Cheyenne Mountain, the Will Rogers Shrine, and the mountains south of town look down on #6011 and the yard crew as #2 arrives at the Santa Fe station and preparations are made to add the three cars. It is a bright January afternoon, with only a hint of the storms which might blow down off the peaks before the day is out.

*(Robert W. Andrews)*

Perhaps the greatest changes in life around what was then Colorado's second largest city were brought about by World War II, for several large military installations, most notably Camp (later Fort) Carson and Peterson Field, were constructed there. In addition to a large amount of freight business, their presence brought to Colorado Springs a large number of senior officers who, like General Palmer before them, fell in love with the location, the climate, and the scenery. Consequently, at the end of hostilities not only were the existing bases retained and enlarged, but the Air Force chose it as the headquarters of the nation's air defense, and also to be the site of the Air Force Academy.

*(Above)* While such installations did, with the exception of Fort Carson to whom the Army constructed a six mile branch, not bring in a great deal of freight business, they did generate considerable passenger business, as here when Missouri Pacific PA #8007 sweeps into town eastbound in August, 1961, to pick up a crowd of military personnel, returning vacationers, and ordinary citizens on their way to points east. The COLORADO EAGLE, was a popular train for business originating here, and was the Rio Grande's second-highest grossing passenger train. In peak season it required the services of a helper conductor to ensure that all the Colorado Springs tickets were picked up before arrival at Pueblo some 45 miles and 50 minutes later.

*(Opposite page, top)* The other railroad in the area most closely associated with the Rio Grande was the Rock Island, which maintained a joint agency and at one time operated its passenger trains to Pueblo and Denver over its trackage. The last transcontinental to enter the state, it arrived in 1888 and was formally abandoned in 1980. For many years it operated the only through Colorado Springs-Chicago service not requiring patrons to change trains enroute, a convenience greatly appreciated. This is shown here at the joint station on Bastille Day (July 14) of 1955 as #636 heads a six car Colorado Springs section of THE ROCKY MOUNTAIN ROCKET loading passengers for its noon departure against a background of towering mountains and a bit of freight activity. Such scenes will become more and more infrequent as the ROCKET dwindles in importance, the E7s take on an economy paint scheme, and Chicago-Colorado Springs dining and sleeper service are dropped.

*(Opposite page, bottom)* Despite the increasing business generated by the presence of the military, the GE 44 tonners continued to protect switching during the 1950s. On the same day in 1955, the 1941-built #38 prepares to exert its 26,400 pound tractive effort to switching a GS gon of coal as Pikes Peak provides an impressive background. The GE has nine more years left on Rio Grande property, before being sold to an equipment broker for eventual service at a Great Lakes Carbon plant in St. Louis. Incidentally, what can the first of the D&RGW GE's do to properly celebrate Bastille Day in "Little London?"

*(Above - Ross B. Grenard, opposite page, both - Grenard Collection)*

(*Opposite page, top*) In the 1960s, the VO 660s began taking over the Colorado Springs switcher's chores and so we find one on January 15, 1965, preparing to attach the DENVER ZEPHYR cars to #2. The neat Tudor-style depot of the Santa Fe which had served the Colorado Midland and where once trains departed for and arrived from Cripple Creek stands in the background, complete with spacious waiting room, one-time Harvey House, and railroad offices on the second and third floors. After adding the cars, the 1941 Baldwin will couple onto the string of freight cars and haul them back around the horn to the Rio Grande yard. Traded to EMD on the first order of SD45s, the 72 will have served the railroad for over a quarter-century.

(*Opposite page, bottom*) After utilizing homemade 0-8-0s (2-8-0s with the pony truck amputated) and sampling a variety of diesel products, the Santa Fe decided to follow the D&RGW's suit and use a 44 tonner. In May of 1964, #464, lettered as per the joint facilities agreement with the Colorado and Southern is shown awaiting assignment on the Santa Fe side of town. As a rule, road freight crews handled pick ups and set outs, which made the goat's role less demanding here.

(*Above*) After the end of passenger service on the Joint Line coincident with the coming of Amtrak, it was decided to abandon operations over the Santa Fe through Colorado Springs. One factor in this were the number of residential grade crossings within the city over which northbound trains had to pass, the increase in size of trains, particularly empty BN coal movements, and an adamant refusal by municipal authorities to allow crossing whistles. As a consequence, the northbound trackage was taken up from a point near Crews to Palmer Lake and CTC installed on remaining Rio Grande trackage. Thus, scenes like this of Rio Grande #5571 preparing to head a passenger special north out of the Santa Fe station are but a memory, and as likely to recur as a Colorado Springs and Cripple Creek District 2-8-0 backing in to embark passengers on the trip which Theodore Roosevelt said "bankrupts the English language." In a little while the communication signal will beep twice, the throttle will be latched out, and the 567s will begin to move the 14 car train up the 1% grade in a scene now as dated as any recorded by William Henry Jackson or L.C. McClure.

(*Opposite page, top and above - Robert W. Andrews, opposite page, bottom - Ross B. Grenard*)

# Pueblo

For many years the second largest city in Colorado, largest industrial complex between the Missouri River and the Pacific Coast, and lowest in altitude of any major city on Colorado's eastern slope (4672), Pueblo had a decidedly different personality than did either Denver or Colorado Springs. Whereas Denver took pride in the fact that its economy was more service than manufacturing and Colorado Springs gloried in its "Newport in the Rockies" appellation, Pueblo was, in earlier days, the "Pittsburgh of the West." Gritty, smoky, blue collar and proud of it, it was the home of Colorado Fuel and Iron, the Rio Grande's largest shipper until the late 1950s, and was a major freight interchange point for the railroads serving the city. In fact, of all the D&RGW's bridge line partners, the Mopac interchange at Pueblo contributed the most tonnage during the 1940-1970 period.

*(Above)* The most prominent railroad landmark in the "Steel City" was its Union Station, constructed in 1889 and still extant as these words are written. It was operated by the Pueblo Union Railway and Depot Company for the four railroads operating passenger service to or through town. Here a little bit of the action is shown as THE TEXAS ZEPHYR arrives, a Santa Fe E8m stands by, and Rio Grande equipment is everywhere present on a sunny afternoon in September 1964.

*(Opposite page, top)* Switching at Pueblo was demanding, and for that reason it was to a large extent entrusted to GPs, RS3s, and in some cases, six-axle units. It consisted largely of interchanging blocks of cars or in some cases whole trains between the Rio Grande, Santa Fe, and Missouri Pacific (for whom the D&RGW handled all switching), or lugging iron ore, coal, limestone, and scrap up 2 1/2 miles of 1.4% to CF&I at Minnequa. (In steam, the Rio Grande used 2-10-2s and even ex-N&W 2-8-8-2s in this service.)

In the scene here, GP7 #5107 is shown between assignments, posed against the levee constructed by the Pueblo Flood Control District to help channelize the Arkansas River and prevent another disaster like the flood which devastated the city in June 1921. Not only did that disaster cause some $3,000,000 damage to the railroad and its facilities, but in a bit of political log rolling, Pueblo received flood protection and Denver was authorized to create the Moffat Tunnel Improvement District - that however, is a different story. In any case, do note the cinders covering the bank of the dike, left by several generations of steam engines which passed this way.

*(Above - Vicktor Laszlow, opposite page, top - Wesley L. Haas)*

(Below)  As a major eastern terminal and yard, Pueblo had a 51 stall roundhouse, which saw considerable activity over the years.  It was retained until the late '60's and handled some of the minor repairs to the diesel fleet.  On the last day of 1959, it saw #5624 poking its blue flagged nose into the winter sunshine as its B unit, probably #5623 received a spot of work, before they were sent back west over Tennessee Pass or off to Trinidad with some coal empties for loading at the CF&I mines there.  *(Vicktor Laszlow)*

# THE ROYAL GORGE at Pueblo

Until 1949, Trains #1 and 2 THE ROYAL GORGE did considerable switching on the trackage between the old station and the levee, for through pullmans and coaches were interchanged with the Mopac during its half hour layover, and Denver-Pueblo cars were cut in and out. By 1952 the Mopac's connection was but a memory, but even without the activity of past years it was still quite an occasion as here in April 1952 #5484 sweeps in among the numerous signs of activity present. In the meantime, #1 prepares to depart, having switched out the consist of the SAN LUIS at right, for the trip to Alamosa.

*(Ross Grenard)*

Thirteen years later, in August 1965, the arrival of #2 was by contrast an event most melancholy. The two trains operated only from Denver to Salida, and were not turned there as no yard crew was on duty. The mail and express business had largely vanished, as had such amenities as Denver-Ogden sleeper and dining service. The Pueblo station itself was rapidly losing its commercial and operating importance to a city now more concerned with Interstate Highways and improved air service. The only things which remained as before were the yard lights looking down on the D&RGW-MP yard.
*(Lloyd Stagner)*

# Pueblo to Tennessee Pass

From the yard limit at Pueblo, to the Continental Divide at the summit of Tennessee Pass is a 142.03 mile trip with an increase in total elevation of 5549 feet. During these miles the railroad follows the Arkansas River to within some 20 miles of its source, and sees the scenery change from prairie bluffs and wasteland to alpine meadow presided over by the most lofty of Colorado's 14,000 foot peaks. This is perhaps the most historic of all Rio Grande trackage for it was here between mileposts 160 and 176 that there occurred the confrontation forever known to railroad historians as "The Royal Gorge War." A discussion of the conflict and its eventual resolution are beyond the scope of this book and it is perhaps enough to note that as of the time frame dealt with here, the Santa Fe was operating its Pueblo-Canon City wayfreight over trackage that was then the 2nd subdivision of the D&RGW Pueblo Division.

*(Above)* Coming out of Pueblo on a fine afternoon in September 1968, #3050, last of the railroad's GP35s has a roll on train #61 near Swallows and along a now placid Arkansas River which has in years past harassed the line with more freshets and flooding than any other watercourse in its territory. This is to change soon for the train is passing early indications that the Corps of Engineers will soon begin constructing a new flood control dam which will necessitate a line change to higher ground. This was one of the first stretches of the Rio Grande mainline to receive block signals back in 1928 as the then-management strove to overcome the decades of deferred maintenance resulting from the Western Pacific fiasco. One of the original color lights can be seen next to the piggyback car in the consist. It is also rare, for the GP35s were demoted to B units in 1972, and were no longer used on the point of freight trains.

*(Vicktor Laszlow)*

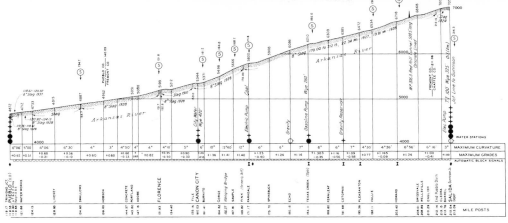

At Canon City, the mountains begin to close in again around the railroad just prior to its entering the defiles of the Royal Gorge. Still, the seat of Fremont County and site of the Colorado State Penitentiary seems less a mountain town than those which lie ahead. In addition, Canon City was the locale of some of the earliest coal mines to be served by the railroad. It also was the site of a major smelter during the Cripple Creek boom. Located at 5344 feet above sea level it is the beginning of the 1% grades on the Royal Gorge Route. At one time it was the junction with the Grape Creek Branch, constructed as a narrow gauge line in 1881 to serve the silver mines of the Wet Mountain valley. It was washed out in 1889, and replaced in 1900 by a standard gauge line from Texas Creek to Westcliffe, which was abandoned in 1938.

*(Below)* In July of 1957, an RS3 was in charge of the local from Pueblo, and here is shown engaged in setting out a B&O "wagon top" boxcar before heading home. Canon City has remained for many years the turnaround point for the local, as there is little business between here and Salida or even Leadville.
*(Vicktor Laszlow)*

# Royal Gorge

Since it first acquired the track through the defile from Col. Holiday's railroad in the negotiations ending hostilities, and began operating through to Salida, the Royal Gorge has been a staple of promotions. George Beam posed presidents, financiers, and performers in its depths, and the list of sophisticated travelers who were entranced by it is immense and includes both Roosevelts, and countless others from throughout the world who viewed it from regular or special trains - including on several occasions the passengers on the CALIFORNIA ZEPHYR whose trains were routed that way due to problems on the regular route. In our times, Otto Roach, a renowned Denver photographer was retained by the Rio Grande to portray its passenger trains at various times, and two are shown.

*(Opposite page)* In 1947, as things returned to normal after World War II, Roach used his 8x10 view camera to show burly Baldwin #1800, doyen of the last five passenger engines ordered by the road, flying green flags on First #1 as it pauses to let the passengers look over the scenery. Soon the 4-8-4 will whistle in the flag (in itself an audio experience like unto Sir Arthur Sullivan's *Lost Chord*) and its 67,200 pound tractive effort will begin moving its nine pullman green cars up the 1.4 % grade and around the 12 degree curves that are very much a part of *America's Best Loved Travel Wonder*.

*Now, the see-all Vista-Dome car adds thrilling perspective to make the Royal Gorge a brand new travel delight.*

*(Page 1)* Five years later, the scene had changed. The eternal rocks were very much the same, and the suspension bridge still towered 1,000 feet above the rushing waters, but the whole character of #1 had changed. EMD had supplanted Baldwin, and new "Grande Gold" and silver stainless steel had supplanted pullman green. Both the WP and the Missouri Pacific had given up the ghost on connecting trains, and only a Denver-Ogden sleeper or two catered to the affluent tourist who wished to see this fabled attraction from Pullman windows. The brass-railed observations, both the Rio Grande's own and Mr. Pullman's 10 section variety were gone, replaced by an ex-C&O dome round-end modified to operate mid-train. The diners, whose stock in trade was mountain trout, had been replaced with grill-lounges whose menu was less sophisticated. However, even in its power, the ROYAL GORGE does show a bit of individuality today, for leading it is #5481, which became a celebrity of sorts after its 1950 plunge into Gore Canon. For it was rebuilt by La Grange with an F7 carbody, and became the first unit to be painted in what was to become the standard paint scheme. In any event, the unit graced the Grande's timetable for several years, teamed with the earliest scene of the two "CZs" meeting in Glenwood Canon behind PAs painted in the short-lived Orange and Silver image.

*(Above)* In another perspective, PA #6013 is shown on the hanging bridge in April of 1963, as its passengers contemplate the infinite.

*(Opposite page, both - Otto Roach Photo, D&RGW Collection, Western History Department, Denver Public Library, above - Wesley L. Haas)*

*(Opposite page, top)* Years after regular passenger service through the Gorge ended, on October 15, 1971 the *Action Railroad* hosted a Department of Transportation test train engaged in some track geometry work. On the way back from Ogden, it passed through with the business car "Wilson Mc-Carthy" on the rear, and of course made the traditional ten minute pause to see the sights. So here are a group of assorted FRA officials, technicians, and the railroad's engineering staff making like ordinary tourists or VIPs of old.

*(Opposite page, bottom)* The first storm clouds of winter are starting to gather as another GP35 heads east at Howard with the MWM train for the Missouri Pacific. By 1965, the Rio Grande was starting to expand its new concept of short freights to Tennessee Pass and #3033 is leading a quartet of second generation units on 47 cars as they follow the 1.24% through the canon country of central Colorado to points east.

*(Above)* Nearing Salida the canon opens out into verdant valley bordered by the Sangre DeCristos on the south and the Park Range on the north. Here on a lush October 5, 1964 afternoon #5714 is in charge of five F7s hurrying up the valley with 82 cars of manifest freight #77. As the strong afternoon sun glints off the lead unit the crew can relax for their journey is about over.
*(Opposite page, top - James L. Ozment, opposite page, bottom Robert W. Andrews, above - Lloyd A. Stagner)*

# Salida

In July 1955, Salida was still very much in the narrow gauge business and the ROYAL GORGE was still a respectable train compared to what was to come. Even though the 1950s had lessened Salida's importance to narrow gauge operations, the Monarch Branch was extremely busy supplying the limestone for Pueblo's blast furnaces.

*(Above)* In the scene here, PA #6011 leads a seven car train into the station with the narrow gauge line shown taking off to the south and west. The coal chute still stands, as does part of the roundhouse and the old narrow gauge shops. While their numbers have been decimated, there are still a few narrow gauge cars in the yard, and hopefully some passengers and a bit of head end business for the train to pick up during its ten minute stop.

*(Opposite page, both)* This would be the final year for the standard gauge steam here, with 2-8-0s like #1169, shown here in the now largely abandoned engine servicing area beside the narrow gauge shop, and #1173, posed against the snow capped Sangre DeCristos, working in the capacity of extra yard engines, often shuffling narrow gauge gondolas or hauling them off to the barrel transfer. All switchers at Salida and Alamosa were equipped with dual-gauge couplers for such activity.

*(Above & opposite page, top - Grenard Collection, opposite page, bottom- Vicktor Laszlow)*

## Adjusted Tonnage Ratings And Car Limits

| FROM | TO | Class F-9 GP-9 577 5001-5054 Tons | Class FT-P-7 540-547 549-551 555-576 Tons | Class F-3 552-554 Tons | Class SD-7-9 5300-5314 Tons | Class GP-7 RB-3 5100-5113 5200-5204 Tons | Adjustment Factor Tons |
|---|---|---|---|---|---|---|---|
| Denver | East Portal | 920 | 850 | 630 | 1350 | 800 | 3 |
| Tabernash | Winter Park | 950 | 890 | 675 | 1400 | 885 | 4 |
| Orestod | Tabernash | 1760 | 1630 | 1255 | 2600 | 1655 | 6 |
| Orestod | Toponas | 920 | 850 | 630 | 1350 | 800 | 3 |
| Phippsburg | Toponas | 1190 | 1100 | 750 | 1650 | 1200 | 4 |
| Phippsburg | Pallas | 1760 | 1625 | 1250 | 2600 | 1900 | 6 |
| Haybro | Phippsburg | 1190 | 1100 | 750 | 1550 | 1200 | 4 |
| Steamboat | Haybro | 1700 | 1575 | 1200 | 2600 | 1900 | 6 |
| Craig | Steamboat | 3400 | 3150 | 2400 | 4300 | 3550 | 9 |
| Pueblo | Portland | 3500 | 3350 | | 4000 | 3350 | 9 |
| Portland | Canon City | 3350 | 3200 | | 3800 | 3200 | 6 |
| Canon City | Salida | 1500 | 1390 | 1060 | 2000 | 1390 | 4 |
| Salida | Tennessee Pass | 1325 | 1225 | 900 | 1900 | 1200 | 4 |
| **Minturn | Tennessee Pass | 595 | 550 | 390 | 900 | 512 | 2 |
| Grand Jct. | Glenwood | 2025 | 1875 | 1500 | 3100 | 1800 | 6 |
| Glenwood | Minturn | 1400 | 1300 | 975 | 2050 | 1250 | 6 |
| Glenwood | Bond | 1500 | 1400 | 1100 | 2150 | 1400 | 6 |
| Glenwood | Leon | 1700 | 1650 | | | 1650 | 2 |
| Leon | Aspen | 850 | 800 | | | 800 | 2 |
| Malta | Eilers | 700 | 680 | | | 650 | 2 |
| Eilers | Leadville | 600 | 550 | | | 550 | 2 |
| Salida | Mayville | 800 | 750 | | 1100 | 750 | 2 |
| Mayville | Monarch | 380 | 340 | | 530 | 340 | 1 |

**Units 6001-6013 Rated 430 tons each unit, Minturn to Tennessee Pass.
**Units 5462-3-4 Rated 320 tons each unit, Minturn to Tennessee Pass.

Tonnage ratings shown for all locomotives are based on single unit. Where more than one unit is used tonnage will be based on number of units used. Where different class units are used in a locomotive, either as train engine or in helping service, the rating of the lowest rated unit will govern the rating of all units on that train.

Following are the car limits per train Tennessee Pass to Minturn—4 or more units:
    90 loaded cars.
    100 loads and empties mixed.
    100 empties.

Following are the car limits per train Tennessee Pass to Salida:
    Eastward freight trains handled by 4 or more units—Tennessee Pass to Malta—110 cars. Malta to Salida—120 cars.

Eastward trains between Salida and Pueblo handled by locomotive of 3 or more units may handle not over 120 cars, mixed loads and empties. With locomotive consisting of 2 units Class FT-F7, not over 80 cars. A single unit FT-F7 may handle not over 40 cars.

Locomotive consisting of two Class GP-SD units may handle same as 3 or more Class FT-F7 units. A single unit Class GP-SD may handle 60 cars.

Do not handle more than 90 cars of rock or heavier loading with locomotive consisting of 4 or more units Class FT-F7.

# Monarch Branch

*(Opposite page, top)* In an overview from the top of Tenderfoot Mountain, Train #2 is shown departing for Pueblo in June of 1956 against a background of the Sangre De Cristos and amid the desolation of shop buildings, a soon to be demolished coal chute, and empty spaces where once the narrow gauge yards were prominent. Crews are already at work on the standard gauging of the Monarch Branch, and soon the whistles of the narrow gauge locomotives will echo no more across the valley. Both Salida and the passenger train have a decade or so to go in service, but neither will survive the changes which are to come in the next years.

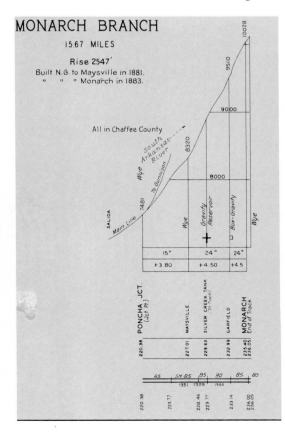

MONARCH BRANCH

15.67 MILES

Rise 2547'

Built N.G. to Maysville in 1881.
" " " Monarch in 1883.

All in Chaffee County

*(Opposite page, bottom)* Where once the narrow gauge mainline headed west to challenge Marshall Pass and to roll beside the waters of the Gunnison through its Black Canon, two GP30s head for Monarch Quarry and the 4.5% grades which lie between Salida and the source of CF&I's limestone. In the background Tenderfoot Mountain, its overlook, and the high school student's block "S" look down on the activities. On this fall day, the EMDs turbochargers will likely come in handy at the 10,028 foot altitudes which lie ahead. In the years before abandonment it was standard for the Monarch train to come out of Pueblo with two Geeps, make the Monarch run, do such switching as needed doing at Salida, and then head home with several dozen gons. While this might have seemed boring to those who had watched the operation in earlier days, it was still fascinating to see the adoption of modern technology to an operation so recently anachronistic.

*(Above)* The 1956 standard-gauging of the Monarch Branch was an engineering feat carried out in-house by the railroad in a relatively short period of time. That they managed to standard gauge such spots as the Garfield Switchback, shown here, required a high degree of skill by both the engineers who planned it and the MofW forces who carried it out. There were some mistaken assumptions such as using SD7s which were, after this test run of August 27, 1956, abandoned.

*(Opposite page, top and above - Vicktor Laszlow, opposite page, bottom - Ed Fulcomer)*

*(Opposite page, top)*  The first standard gauge train to traverse the branch after completion of the track work is shown here on August 23, 1956 behind #111 tiptoeing through the meadows west of Poncha Junction.  Here, still sporting its dual-gauge couplers, the 1943 Alco heads back to Salida after loading some of the rail which required replacement along the line.

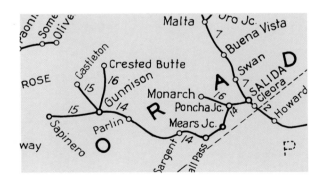

*(Opposite page, bottom)*  Even using dynamic brakes, pressure retaining valves, and a modern air brake technology far more advanced than any available to engineers in the narrow gauge era, getting a train of any size downgrade was a difficult task as shown here where #5944 and #5952 ease a train of loads downhill near Maysville.  The Monarch Branch was partly a victim of the playing out of its mineral deposits and partially of changes within steel technology.  Nonetheless it was an interesting part of operations and without it Salida's importance to the railroad was greatly diminished.

*(Above)*  As the first storm clouds of an August afternoon in 1956 begin to gather, the ROYAL GORGE unloads mail and changes crews before heading up the Arkansas Valley.  The Red Devil coal loader once used to feed the tenders of the 4-8-4s stands silent and unused beside the track as #5541 waits impatiently to get out of town.  The changeover of the Monarch Branch is in its final stages, and for all practical purposes Salida is now strictly a 4' 8 1/2" operation.  Yet the gathering clouds symbolically portend what lies ahead for both the train and the town.  For within a decade Salida will see an end to railroading as it had known it since the Rio Grande founded it in 1880.  Passenger service, assigned yard power, the physical facilities of railroading, even the company hospital and Salida's status as a division point will all be lost forever, and only the memories will remain.

*(Opposite page, top and above - Vicktor Laszlow, opposite page, bottom - Ed Fulcomer)*

(*Opposite page, top*) It was these facilities and the desire to immortalize them on film which prompted the photographer to climb to the top of the coaling facilities on June 20, 1956 and make this cloudy day portrait looking toward the Continental Divide. In the foreground 3-rail trackage shines in the misty sunlight and the main leads off towards the summit of Mt. Princeton on which the sun still shines. Today Salida is desolate with nothing left to show its one-time importance to the railroad.

(*Opposite page, bottom*) Few things could better illustrate the decline of Salida's importance than the fate which befell its last passenger train, from the exemplification of the era to the pathetic remnant shown here on one of its last trips in 1967, amid the desolation in the remnants of a once major terminal.

(*Above*) And in a similar pose, on November 9, 1958 during the last few years that it technically ran through to Salt Lake, #1 was but a shadow of itself totaling but four cars, before finally succumbing. Here it stands in the late afternoon sunshine, beside a deserted station platform, in an image which recalls for all time the final end of an era.

Today, the Royal Gorge has become a main artery for the freight trains of a new railroad. And as they roll through Salida without stopping, one wonders if anyone is aware, or will be aware in future years, that they are treading on hallowed ground?
(*All - Vicktor Laszlow*)

# Leadville

*(Above)* In the last few months that it ran west of Salida, #'s 1&2 averaged only three cars, and if it possessed any legitimate reason for existence it rode in the RPO car. It was still a pretty little train and made a fine picture in the October 1964 sunlight, even if #6013 and #6003, were beginning to show their years. Of all the passenger units operated by the railroad, they were some of the only ones not to enjoy a paint job, and to be retired still wearing the 1952 five stripe image. Only one of the six ever was redone in the 1960s single stripe scheme.

*(Opposite page, top)* Fifty-five miles up the Arkansas, #1 is shown again slowing for its stop at Malta on July 17, 1956. Here the branch to the "Cloud City" took off over what had once been the narrow gauge over 11,000 foot Fremont Pass to the riches of the Blue River Mining District. At this time, the branch no longer served such elevated locales as Ibex or California Gulch and existed only to provide a connection for the Colorado & Southern's isolated Climax Spur, and to serve American Smelting and Refining's Arkansas Valley smelter.

*(Opposite page, bottom)* In the 1880s Leadville was producing mineral wealth on a scale unprecedented to most of the world, and was the goal of countless railroads whose names have ben lost to history. As it was, its battlements were scaled only by the Rio Grande, the South Park, and the Colorado Midland. Of these sucessor C&S survived operating a truncated line to Climax and the Grande was represented on May 31, 1965 by one GP9, a wooden caboose that had seen better days and a freight house last painted during World War II.

*(Above - Lloyd Stagner, opposite page, top - Vicktor Laszlow, opposite page, bottom John Buvinger, Laszlow collection)*

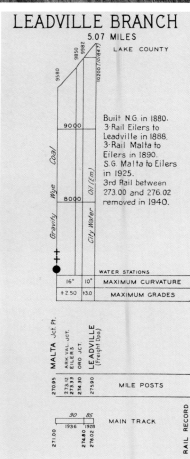

# Tennessee Pass

While the eastern slope at Tennessee Pass is a gradual one, and exceeds 1.4% only for two short stretches, the western approach up Eagle River Canon has been, since its construction in 1890 a major operating problem for at least four generations of railroaders. Its unremitting 3% grade, its frigid temperatures and high percentage of heavy bulk traffic have all combined to create a fascination and a fear among railroaders that is only now beginning to abate. During our times, Rio Grande management has considered the abandonment of the line between Canon City and Malta, has rerouted heavy coal trains over the Moffat Line to avoid the excessive crew costs entailed in operating up to nine unit helper sets out of Minturn, and made other similar efforts. As a result of the SP merger most freight from the northwest and central California now moves this way to connect with the "Cotton-Rock" line via trackage rights over the former Mopac Pueblo line, so that has added a new dimension to the equation. In any event, the twenty odd miles from Minturn to the tunnel are quite a railroad, regardless of the motive power involved.

*(Opposite page, top)* Our journey will begin at the 10,221 foot east portal of the 2550 foot long tunnel finished in 1945 to replace the original tunnel constructed in the 1890s to supplant the narrow gauge line operating over the top.

*(Opposite page, bottom)* At the tunnel's west portal, a mixed lash up of first and second-generation units heads back to Minturn for fueling and another train to help in a ritual performed since operations began here. In steam days the dispatcher combined several helpers and sent them down the hill as one movement, thus saving track space during rush periods. In August 1971, all the units are MU'd, so it is a little easier.

*(Above)* During the fall of 1953, #3601 exerts its 131,000 pound tractive effort on the last mile into the Summit Tunnel on a "Malta Turn." By this time almost all through freight was being moved by F7s, and by the first part of 1954 regeared FTs would be available for helper service and these turns operated out of Minturn handling tonnage for Leadville and the Arkansas Valley smelter. Since #3601's trailing consist appears to be coke or coal it is a good assumption that that's what it is. It took a good deal of tractive effort to boost these trains up the hill and it is a pretty good assumption that one or even two 3600s are cut in as helpers.

*(Opposite page, top - Grenard Collection, opposite page, bottom - Robert W. Andrews, above - Don Ball Collection)*

# 3600s

*(Opposite page)* On a bitterly cold day in March 1947, Train #2's 4-8-4 is boosted up the hill at Mitchell by #3604. While perhaps lacking the definition of some photographs, this does show very effectively the "mystique" of this stretch of railroad in that era. #2 is only nine cars today, but the Rio Grande is taking no chances on frozen journals or steam lines, and the billowing bituminous exhausts stand in the sharp crisp air to attest to that.

*(Above)* Were merchandise freights any easier to get up hill? Yes and no, as here in 1954 #5611 with its throttle in the 8th notch and slack stretched overcomes the inertia of some ninety-nine cars. Two 3600s recently reactivated during the fall 1954 rush are doing their part quite smokily. This was the last year for steam out of Minturn, and R.H. Kindig, peering into his postcard *Graphlex* in the foreground is recording the scene for posterity.
*(Opposite page - Charles Kerrigan, above - Ross B. Grenard)*

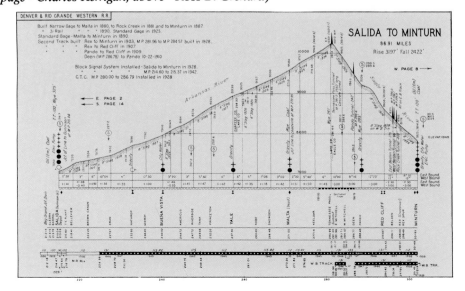

AUTOMATIC BLOCK SIGNALS

*(Opposite page, top)* The ex N&W Y2s purchased during World War II were intended to supplement Rio Grande power in helper assignments and this is just what #3552, ex-N&W 1724, Baldwin 1919) is doing as it assists a 3600 uphill on a train of Utah iron ore. The 10,220 foot elevation at Tennessee Pass is the highest which any of the illustrious Y family will ever reach, and #3552 is the last of all fifteen in active service on mainline grades. After 1949, dieselization will enable the Rio Grande to replace such compounds with 3600s in helper service and the last of class L-109 will be stricken from the roster in 1950. Although too slow for mainline freight elsewhere, the 1919 Baldwins did render effective support on grades like this.

*(Opposite page, bottom)* In July 1965, #5771 was just another "covered wagon" as it headed east through Mitchell with the ASPDF, bound for Pueblo and a Mopac connection. No less than five F units are deployed to keep this, one of the fastest eastbounds on the railroad on schedule. According to the then current timetable, the ASPDF was due out of Ogden at 12:30 AM, Minturn at 12:55 PM, and delivered its cars to the MP at 9:00 that evening.

One factor which cannot be stressed enough is the importance placed on the SP interchange at Ogden, even in those days. For the freight tonnage and revenues received from the SP was two to three times that from the WP. The track immediately to the right of #5771 is the passing track at Mitchell, once part of the double track installed early in the century to cope with congestion and rendered redundant by the 1959 CTC installation.

*(Above)* In another view of the helper set, this time from the rear, it drops downhill near Mitchell on a fine summer afternoon. The exotic combinations used on helper sets as here were an interesting aspect of Rio Grande diesel operations during the transition period between cab and hood units. Since all the Fs had, by this time, been equipped with nose plugs some remarkable combinations could be obtained.

*(Opposite page, top - Robert Le Massena, opposite page, bottom - Vicktor Laszlow, above - Robert W. Andrews)*

# Pando

*(Below)* At Pando, where the unremitting 3% flattened out ever so slightly, #3093 eases its train to a halt preparatory to setting out a bulldozer for some MW program. The site of Camp Hale, opened during World War II to train the 10th Mountain Division, Pando is located in a valley called Eagle Park in earlier days. During the war, activity was so intense on the railroad that the smoke pall was enough to cause shutdowns of all military activities for long periods. This is not the case today, for both road engine and helper are EMD products. In this October scene, the aspen are changing, the storm clouds are beginning to gather and soon the first snow will begin to fall in the high, desolate, and inhospitable area.

*(Ronald C. Hill, Grenard Collection)*

# Eagle River Canyon

*(Opposite page)* Located at the upper end of the Eagle River's spectacular canon, Redcliff has always been a popular photographic location, for it offers a variety of angles and the trains to make them effective. In our first scene, four GP30s lead an 83 car eastbound out of the Canon in a scene from near Highway 24. Deep in the consist some five F7s are grinding away up hill.

*(Robert W. Andrews)*

Twenty two years earlier things were different as F7s relied on the aid of 2-8-8-2s such as #3400, a 1913 compound still sporting a green boiler jacket as was the wont of the paint shops on occasion, and #3613, one of the 1930 Alco simple articulateds, unkempt and in need of a trip to the paint shop after too many trips through too many tunnels. In any case the pair have left the canon so smoky that it will take awhile for it to clear.

*(Ross B. Grenard)*

## TONNAGE RATINGS AND CAR LIMITS

These ratings are the usual tonnage ratings for dead freight trains. Chief Dispatchers are authorized to increase or decrease these ratings in their discretion in accordance with standing instructions, to adjust for slack grades, condition of power, necessity for maintaining stock schedules, or for any other reasons which justify.

In computing tonnage, the adjustment factor represents the number of tons, which shall be added to the total weight of each car loaded or empty. The caboose shall count as a car. Tonnage hauled may exceed the rating by a fraction of a car.

Following are the car limits per train Tennessee Pass to Minturn:
   90 loaded cars.
   100 loads and empties mixed.
   100 empties.

Following are the car limits per train, Sunnyside Branch:
   Sunnyside to Columbia Junction: 50 loaded cars. Any empties may be handled in addition to loads. Trains handled by diesel electric switch engines: 40 loaded cars, not to exceed 30 cars of coal; empties may be handled in addition to loads. Caboose must be on train and air coupled thru at Sunnyside before final air test is made prior to departure.

   Columbia Junction to Mounds: 105 cars.

# Adjusted Tonnage Ratings

| FROM | TO | Class 5400 H.P. Diesels 540, 541, 543-547, 549-551 | Class 5400 H.P. Diesels 542, 548 | Class 6000 H.P. Diesels 552-554 | Class L-131 L-132 Engines 3600-3619 | Class L-109 Engines 3550-3564 | Class L-107 Engines 3500-3509 | Class L-105 Engines 3700-3714 | Class L-95 Engines 3400-3415 xx | Class M-75 Engines 1600-1609 | Class M-68 Engines 1800-1804 | Class M-64 x M-67 Engines 1501-1510 1520-1530 1700-1713 | Class K-59 Engines 1200-1213 | Class C-48 Engines 1131-1199 | Class C-41 Engines 1000-1028 | Adjustment Factor |
|---|---|---|---|---|---|---|---|---|---|---|---|---|---|---|---|---|
|  |  | Tons | Tons | Tons | Tons | Tons | Tons | Tons | Tons | Tons | Tons | Tons | Tons | Tons | Tons | Tons |
| Salida | Tennessee Pass | 3500 | 2800 | 3600 | 3000 | 2700 | 2650 | 2650 | 2000 | 1800 | 1580 | 1600 | 1210 | 1070 | 940 | 4 |
| Minturn | Tennessee Pass | 1450 | 1400 | 1550 | 1350 | 1125 | 1100 | 1100 | 950 | 780 | 620 | 685 | 550 | 450 | 420 | 2 |
| Grand Jct | Glenwood | 6300 | 5300 | 5900 | 5100 |  | 4850 | 4500 | 3700 | 3350 | 3220 | 3000 | 2400 | 2000 | 1750 | 6 |
| Glenwood | Minturn | 3800 | 3500 | 3900 | 3300 | 3000 | 2950 | 2650 | 2400 | 2000 | 1870 | 1700 | 1500 | 1200 | 1130 | 4 |
| Glenwood | Bond | 4400 | 4200 | 4400 | 3500 |  |  |  | 2550 |  |  | 1825 | 1600 | 1280 |  | 6 |
| Grand Jct | Mounds | 4700 | 4200 | 4900 | 4400 |  |  |  | 3500 | 2525 | 2400 | 2315 | 1790 | 1630 |  | 5 |
| Mounds | Helper | 4800 | 4400 | 4900 | 4600 |  | 3850 | 3700 | 3400 | 2750 | 2600 | 2500 | 1970 | 1630 |  | 5 |
| Helper | Woodside | 5000 | 4600 | 5100 | 6000 |  | 5300 | 4600 | 4550 | 3670 | 3300 | 3300 | 2390 | 2100 |  | 7 |
| Woodside | Green River | 4800 | 4400 | 5100 | 4400 |  |  | 3700 |  | 3020 | 2600 | 2700 | 2040 | 1870 |  | 6 |
| Green River | Grand Jct | 4700 | 4400 | 5100 | 4400 |  |  | 3550 |  | 2525 | 2400 | 2315 | 1790 | 1630 |  | 5 |
| Mounds | Columbia Jct | | | | 2800 | | 2300 | | 2000 | 1540 | | 1365 | 1050 | 950 | 700 | 3 |
| Columbia Jct | Sunnyside | | | | 1450 | | 1325 | | 1030 | | | | 530 | 450 | 350 | 2 |
| Grand Jct | Delta | | | | | | | | | | | | 4250 | 3320 | 2720 | 10 |
| Delta | Montrose | | | | | | | | | | | | 1950 | 1570 | 1280 | 5 |
| Delta | Somerset | | | | | | | | | | | | 1850 | 1520 | 1240 | 5 |
| Somerset | Rogers Mesa | | | | | | | | | | | | 4000 | 3200 | 2380 | 8 |

xx Tractive effort engines 3400, 3401, 3402, 3403, 3409 and 3414 have been increased to 99,000 pounds and are rated 4.2% more than other 3400 series engines.

x Engine 1515 is M-67 class.

*(Opposite page, top)* By 1965, most of the FT sets had been traded off and it was the turn of the F7s to be bumped down to helper service. At this time the Rio Grande had gone to shorter trains and so less units were needed in a set. So, in August of that year we observe two units pushing behind the caboose of an eastbound manifest in Eagle Canon. Looking very much like a well-detailed HO model, #5644 heads upgrade.

*(Opposite page, bottom)* One of the few industrial shippers on this section of line was the Gilman Mine, located on the canon and working the mineral deposits of Battle Mountain. Operated by a subsidiary of New Jersey Zinc, it was closed permanently in 1985, but not before it became a legendary example of the lengths man will go to in his pursuit of mineral riches. In 1965, it was producing non-ferrous metals and the presence of several Rio Grande box cars indicated that business was good.

*(Above)* Just above Rex, some 5 miles east of Minturn the once double track line encounters the mouth of Eagle Canon and the territory becomes a bit less constricted. Only a few of these miles remain for freight #71 as it makes its way down the grade and into the yard.

*(Opposite page, both - Vicktor Laszlow, above - Ronald C. Hill, Grenard Collection)*

# Minturn

Minturn was named for Thomas Minturn, a Denver and Rio Grande Vice President at the time the line was extended down the Eagle River in 1887. It was a community whose existence was almost totally devoted to the railroad, and for many years its location could best be determined by the pall of smoke sent into the heavens daily by the helpers garrisoned here. All this changed in the 1950s when diesels took over both helper and road service.

**5-B. TENNESSEE PASS TO MINTURN.** Trains consisting of empty cars: retainers will be used on every other car in 10 pound position, alternated at inspection point. When cars are equipped with 4 position release control retaining valve, these retainers will be placed in slow direct exhaust position instead of 10 pound position on empty cars.

Trains consisting of loaded cars: retainers will be used in 20 pound position on all cars having a gross weight of 50 tons or more and in 10 pound position on other loaded cars Tennessee Pass to Pando. Retainers will be used in 10 pound position on all loaded cars Pando to Minturn and in case retaining power is insufficient to hold train while auxiliary reservoirs are being charged, engineman may request that more retaining valves be placed in 20 pound position.

Trains handled by Diesel locomotives having dynamic brake operative on four quarters, beginning at the head end of the train use one retainer in 10 lb. position for each 50 tons in excess of 1550 actual tons; locomotives with dynamic brake operative on three quarters, beginning at the head end of the train use one retainer in 10 lb. position for each 50 tons in excess of 1000 actual tons.

Trains handled by Diesel locomotives with dynamic brake operative on less than three quarters, retaining valves must be handled in the same manner as prescribed in special timetable rules for trains handled with steam locomotives.

*(Above)* Consequently, Minturn's atmosphere began to clear up and by 1965 this view could be recorded from above to show the railroad layout, and the Eagle River's narrow valley west of the area. Much has changed from the steam days, for the roundhouse, the turntable and coal dock are now gone.

*(Opposite page, top)* Perhaps the changes to Minturn over the years were best illustrated in these two slides taken at the same spot nearly a quarter of a century apart. In the first, on Sept. 3, 1949, a fifteen car ROYAL GORGE has just arrived behind 4-8-4 #1800, and amidst the hammering of Alemite guns, takes water and waits for a 3600 to couple on for the stressful trip ahead. In the background, the outbound engineer and conductor check over the massive, smoke-stained Baldwin, and the foreman, attired in white overalls, supervises the proceedings. In a moment, the articulated helper will couple up, the air will be tested, and #2 will move east in a shower of smoke, steam and cinders towards the summit.

*(Opposite page, bottom)* Almost a quarter of a century has past as #3093 set out a car and prepares to take on a helper. Passenger service, steam, and the facilities for servicing steam have long since passed into history. Only the hills are the same, and they will soon echo the chant as yet another Rio Grande train heads east. As these words are written, the word is that a new name will be painted on the locomotives passing through Minturn. Yet can a century of valor and accomplishment be erased by a management decision and a coat of paint? The hills have long memories, and at such a passing, even they must mourn the loss.

*(Above - Vicktor Laszlow, opposite page, top - Ross B. Grenard, opposite page, bottom - Ronald C. Hill, Grenard Collection)*

# Alamosa

Alamosa was the spot where the Rio Grande first came into the presence of its namesake river. After the great conversion to standard gauge it became, along with Salida, the easternmost outpost of 3' gauge. Home of the locomotive and car shops, headquarters of the empire that was the 4th Division of the railroad, it was also the spot where standard gauge steam breathed its last on Dec. 26, 1956. Its roundhouse had serviced both the largest and smallest of the railroad's steam power over the years, and could be a lively place at times when the perishable and livestock business were booming.

*(Above)* Sometimes when business was good and the supply of serviceable standard power in short supply, narrow gauge Mikes were called in on the dual-gauge line down the San Luis Valley to Antonito. Here, #481 is shown using an idler car to get a wheel on an "Antonito Turn" on Sept. 18, 1956, with a covered hopper and four stock cars for a consist. Since the narrow gauge Mikes exerted some 36,000 pounds tractive effort compared to 42,900 for standard gauge 2-8-0s, they could do almost as well. Incidentally, #481 is still in service on the Durango and Silverton, and may well outlive all of the other power shown in this book. Sobering thought, what!

*(Below)* This integration of standard and narrow gauge operations at Alamosa (and Salida before 1956) necessitated the use of switch engines whose coupling capacity embraced both gauges. Consequently Baldwin #73 and several other switchers, including Alcos #110 and 111 were fitted with dual-gauge couplers for use in such yards as Salida and Alamosa. Here #73 is shown idling away next to a 3' gauge caboose in October of 1966.
*(Above - Ross B. Grenard, below - Ed Fulcomer)*

Commencing about 1950, the L-131s began operating into the San Luis Valley on freights over LaVeta Pass replacing lighter power which had previously been used. This came coincidentally with the increase in business on the narrow gauge caused by pipe traffic bound for points on the narrow gauge and the extensive natural gas drilling then beginning.

*(Left)* As a consequence, scenes like this meeting of #3619 and #490 together at Alamosa became regular occurrences for a few years. Here, having their fires cleaned are representatives of the largest engines on both gauges. As large as the 3600s were, it is interesting to note that it does not completely overshadow the Burnham-built 2-8-2. At that time, May 10, 1952, both locomotives were earning their keep and were marked up for freights that afternoon. In addition to such freight as was transferred from the Durango line, the Rio Grande originated considerable traffic out of the San Luis Valley, including perishables, livestock, lumber, and perlite.

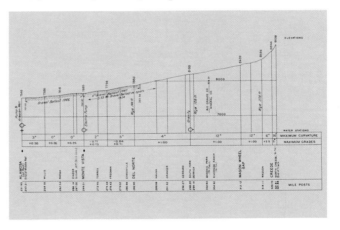

A large amount of this business originated in the fertile agricultural areas on the lower reaches of the 69 mile Creede Branch, but on its upper reaches the only traffic was in livestock and from those Mineral County mines still operating around what had been the richest silver strike in the state. Built as narrow gauge, the Creede Branch had been standard gauged in 1901 after discovery of gold gave the nearly moribund silver camp a new lease on life.

*(Right)* On Sept. 19, 1956, a combination of outbound ore and seven cars of sheep to be picked up at Wasson resulted in a trip all the way up the line, and here is #1151 (which on December 26, will ring down the curtain on standard gauge steam operations) dropping down the upper reaches of the Rio Grande River above Wagon Wheel Gap. On this placid fall day, it seems difficult to contemplate the intensity of activity once present and that in a few months one of the last ties to the area's past will be forever severed.
*(Both - Ross B. Grenard)*

# The Moffat Line

*Having completed our tour of Rio Grande's original route via the Royal Gorge and Tennessee Pass, we return to Denver to begin a trip west on the Moffat Line.*

*(Above)* The construction of North Yard in 1949 and its effect on the Golden Branch of the Colorado and Southern necessitated granting the C&S trackage rights over the Rio Grande main to C&S Junction, some 4.88 miles west where, waiting for Extra 5641 east to pass is C&S #823, a 1956 SD9, still painted in the original Burlington Lines road-switcher image. #823 is in charge of one of several "Beer Trains" operated daily to haul away the literally train loads of Mr. Coors' Rocky Mountain Spring Water required by its ever rising demand. Spring is in the air on this pleasant day in March of 1967, as the 823 waits for the passage of its host's tonnage and whatever else the Denver dispatcher has coming before resuming its eastbound progress.

*(Opposite page, top)* Getting a run for the 2% grades which lie before it, #5315, first of the SD45s, heads a lash-up of some nine second-generation units. The reason for the elephantine power consist is obscure, but the rather long trailing consist does suggest that two westbound manifests may have been combined to save crew costs. Another is that perhaps a power transfer is being accomplished. In any case, on a December afternoon in 1970, in typical Denver weather, the Rio Grande is expediting freight and is ready for any extremes of weather which lie ahead before the 9239 foot apex of the Moffat Tunnel is reached.

*(Opposite page, bottom)* The siding at Rocky, once named Arena, has several distinctions. It is at the base of "the Big Ten," a loop by which David Moffat's civil engineers succeeded in achieving an elevation of some 500 feet in 3.2 miles while holding to a 2.0% grade and a maximum curvature of 10 degrees. One of the singular achievements of engineering in a state known for them, it has carried trains from the 2-6-6-0s of this upstart railroad to Amtrak's CALIFORNIA ZEPHYR, and is as awe inspiring today, as it was when steam ruled the railroad.

But getting back to Rocky, it was renamed in the 1950s for the Rocky Flats area which it is near and for the Rocky Flats nuclear plant which has achieved considerable notoriety over the years. It is the junction of the spur to the plant, which hosted many special movements over the years, and which was the scene of many a lively anti-war demonstration in the 1960s and 1970s as activists attempted to impede the progress of "Rocky Turns" entering the plant. Rocky has more pleasant connotations though, for it was a flag stop of choice for Boulderites, and residents of the Golden and Arvada areas boarding the "Ski Train" for Winter Park. Here on the morning of March 30, 1968, a crowd waits to board the ex-Northern Pacific coaches of an eighteen car train headed by six F7s. Though the morning is bright and sunny, the capacity load should find conditions to their liking on the slopes over the Continental Divide. Rio Grande ski trains have a long history, and the railroad's role in helping develop the now multi-million dollar industry is a story in itself. In recent years, new equipment has been obtained to upgrade this operation and it appears that the long association is to continue.

*(Above and opposite page, top - James B. Calvert, opposite page, bottom - James L. Ozment)*

# The Big Ten

*(Above)* On the morning of February 8, 1969, with snow on the pilot encountered on the 168 mile trip down from Phippsburg, #5953 eases an MX by the west switch at Rocky, assisted by #5654, and #5307, the latter tagging along and headed for the Burnham Shop. While the old Moffat Line is normally associated with unit coal trains at this date, there is still some general freight including lumber and grain moving out of the Yampa Valley and today's train proves it. In any event, the mountains are behind the markers and the next few miles to North Yard should be a piece of cake. Glinting in the sun just above the first flat of lumber can by seen the aluminum box holding the CTC relays for the west end of Clay siding. It is said that in the pre-CTC days it was customary when eastbound or westbound freights had meets requiring opening the switch at Arena (as it was known then) crewmembers would scramble up or down the hill, stretch their legs, and enjoy a cigar after opening the switch.

*(Opposite page, top)* On July 19, 1950. the Rocky Mountain Railroad Club sponsored a one day circle trip on the Rio Grande, Denver to Denver via the Moffat Tunnel, Dotsero Cutoff, Tennessee Pass and the Royal Gorge. The trip which featured steam all the way and cost the munificent sum of $19.00 is shown here advancing up the Big Ten behind 4-8-4 #1705 and 2-8-8-2 #3618, whose exertions were required to boost the eighteen car train from Denver to East Portal. Here the impeccably polished articulated heads around the first of the 10 degree curves, and the passengers begin to savor what lies ahead of them.

*(Opposite page, bottom)* While its June 10, 1978 date would put it outside the time frame of this volume, Ron Hill's scene of a westbound manifest looped around the second and third curves of the Fireclay Loop is so timeless as to merit inclusion. In this case two GP40s and two six-axle units are leading the train's assortment of auto racks and parts, covered hoppers, and mixed merchandise up the 2% in a scene to recall the memory of all those who engineered, constructed, and operated this, the first of many challenges which lay in the way which had to be dealt with to make the dream of David Moffat a reality. And a salute too, to those who in our lifetimes made this truly the *Main Line Thru The Rockies.*

*(Above and opposite page, bottom - Ronald C. Hill, Grenard Collection, opposite page, top - Ross B. Grenard)*

# THE PROSPECTOR

The postwar PROSPECTOR began service in 1946 between Denver and Salt Lake. It was the creation of and most closely watched by Wilson McCarthy, who both as Trustee and President, reviewed its nightly performance immediately upon arriving at his office. While never an extra-fare train, or one which transported a passenger list containing the names of "the rich and famous" it did prove to all who rode it that (1) good things come in small packages and that (2) the Rio Grande could operate a train to serve the businessman as expertly as any of its competitors.

In the spring of 1948, numbers 7 and 8 were very much a part of the image the railroad sought to project, and it arranged for photographer Roach to record a portrait of it in the beauty of its black and gold tiger stripes. Rather than come up with a new image to doll up the standard weight equipment which was pressed into service on the train, it was decided to repaint the assigned passenger cars in the new diesel scheme.

The result was most pleasing to the eye, as #8 posed at Coal Creek behind #551 A&B, an FT equipped with factory-installed steam generator in the B unit, baggage car #739 (converted by Burnham into a baggage-dormitory for the dining car crew), coach #1002 which dated from the Gould era and which, along with five others, were enhanced, streamlined, and given wide windows for THE EXPOSITION FLYER in 1939. They are followed by diner-lounge *Mt. Massive,* which also dated from that era but which had been upgraded in 1935 and which could be configured as either a full diner, a diner lounge or a buffet car, then, *Penalosa,* a 10 section-2 compartment drawing room sleeper, and finally carrying the markers, *Elm Grove,* a 1948 Calumet rebuild containing 12 roomettes, 2 single and three double bedrooms. Even after making this unscheduled stop, #8 should pull into Denver on the dot at 8:15 AM, much to the joy of Judge McCarthy.

*(Otto Roach Photo, D&RGW Collection, Denver Public Library, Western Collection.)*

# Coal Creek

*(Above)* The highway overpass at Coal Creek is a familiar location to those who have photographed the Rio Grande over the years, and on February 14, 1962, it became the backdrop for the new Krauss-Maffei units as they headed west on a freight. Here, trailing the familiar dynamometer car they follow the serpentine track west to Tunnel #1 around the corner and a half mile away. Only #4002 and #4003 are active today, probably because #4001 is being used on the Southern Pacific, the other diesel-hydraulic operator, which wants to experiment with a four unit set. But today, 8000 horsepower and 2 FTs pushing behind the caboose seem more than adequate for eighty-six cars.

*(Right)* Thirteen years later the KMs are long gone, the hydraulic experiment dead and the railroad's tonnage is in the hands of a horde of second-generation power such as a newly delivered (September 1974) GP40-2, shown here heading downgrade and exiting Tunnel #1 above Coal Creek. With dynamics howling and brake smoke hanging in the frigid air, #3116 leads its fifty-three car consist out of the last of the forty-two tunnels between Bond and Denver.

*(Above - Wesley L. Haas, right - Ross B. Grenard)*

# Plainview

*(Above)* On a pleasant August 21, 1966, #5724 rolled downhill between Plainview and Tunnel #1 with a fifteen car picnic excursion train coming back from Hot Sulphur Springs. During its day as a passenger carrier, the Rio Grande operated these specials quite regularly on Sundays, holidays, and other occasions in the summer. Quite popular with Denverites, they offered an inexpensive and stress-free way to get away to the mountains without having the hassle entailed in mountain driving, and enabled the railroad to utilize otherwise idle equipment. The Moffat Line was always popular for this type of special, and they were operated until the late 1960s.

*(Opposite page, top)* In its final month, THE PROSPECTOR glides through Plainview on a fine spring evening. Re-equipped in 1950 with equipment ordered originally by the C&O, it operated successfully until May 28, 1967, when it was finally doomed by the coming of commercial jets and the losses of the mail contract. Despite this its equipment was meticulously maintained to the end, the service amenities observed, and even in its last year a campaign to market its services undertaken. One of these, although perhaps intangible, was enjoying dinner and breakfast while riding through this territory where, from its windows, the traveler could see almost 1/4 of the state of Colorado.

*(Opposite page, bottom)* While the PROSPECTOR made a fine sight at the beginning and the ending of its nocturnal journey across the Rockies and the Wasatch, and excursion trains were fun and made a lot of friends, it was freight business, either high tariff or high volume, which paid the bills and generated the dividends on the Rio Grande. This business, which was carried on day and night and in all type of weather is exemplified in March of 1963 as GP30s headed by #3008 hold the main at the west end of Plainview's 140-car passing track. As a cold dawn breaks over the gelid scene, the MWMD stands on its dynamic brakes with a 60-car freight of canned goods, new Chevies from Fremont, and Utah lamb enroute to Easter dinner tables.

*(Above - Robert W. Andrews, opposite page, top - James B. Calvert, opposite page, bottom - Roland P. Parsons)*

# The Tunnel District

With Plainview and its breathtaking view of Denver and the "fruited plains" behind it, the railroad enters into twelve miles of steady uphill running, curves of up to 12 degrees, and some twenty-six tunnels, including the infamous Tunnel #10, whose fire back in 1943 cost two lives, forced the diversion of all freight to the Tennessee Pass route, and whose rebuilding figures in every history of the railroad during that period, before reaching Pine Cliff. In a canyon far above the waters of South Boulder Creek, and in an area where man has intruded little, the flanges squeal on the curves and the turbochargers whine as they aspirate the 645s to the fullest. Overcoming the inertia created by a steady 2% becomes the prime law of survival.

*(Opposite page, top)* This is precisely what a brand new #5324 is doing as it heads uphill at Crescent, the access road crossing into the Denver Water Board's Reservoir. After looking at such scenes, one can only wonder what it was like in steam, and where would any company find such men as might make a career of running trains in the face of such obstacles?

*(Opposite page, bottom)* After having traversed the "Tunnel District," #5694 leads 4 units and 41 cars of the PCM around the great curve at Pine Cliff. Here the railroad and the creek come together on the same level and the valley begins to widen out. This is the first human habitation encountered since leaving Plainview and from here on the climb, although steady, is through a mountain valley. Although it is May 2, 1965, the snows of winter still linger at the 7,966 foot altitude as the chant of the 567s echoes off the rocky slopes.

*(Above)* After leaving Pine Cliff eastbound, the YAMPA VALLEY MAIL headed by PA #6003 encounters 76 foot long Tunnel #29 which was and is the most logical way to get through the rocks of the area. Using its dynamics at maximum amperage, the two car train is losing altitude rapidly and will arrive at Denver on the dot. In a few minutes, the passengers will see after exiting Tunnel #3, the panorama of the plains unfold before their eyes as if from an airliner landing. Alas, far too few did, for less than three years later both the train schedule and the big Alcos which protected it were gone.

*(Opposite page, top - James B. Calvert, opposite page, bottom - Lloyd Stagner, above - Robert W. Andrews)*

# Tolland Area

Tolland, so named by the Toll family when they settled in the area, is the last passing siding before East Portal 3.2 miles to the west. Here, too, one comes into the compelling presence of earlier days for it was at Tolland that the Denver, Northwestern and Pacific, later the D&SL added power for the 4% climb up what has become immortalized as the *Giant's Ladder,* to 11,660 foot Rollins Pass. If one looks to the mountain on the right, the rungs, cut into the side of the mountain are plainly visible. It was here that the 2-6-6-0s struggled, 4 to a 24 car train to hoist tonnage over the summit before the tunnel's construction. Today Tolland is a popular place for outings, and picnickers are often surprised to find areas where once the ready tracks stood covered with cinders, and few save those who know, are aware that this was once a busy engine terminal.

*(Above)* During the short time that GP35s were used as leading units, #3036 is shown with an eastbound freight at Tolland awaiting the passage of the westbound CALIFORNIA ZEPHYR. In this March 1965 scene, only a small amount of snow can be seen on the peaks of the Continental Divide, but a sharp eyed reader should have no difficulty finding the *Giant's Ladder* on the hills to the right.

*(Below)* There are no more hills to climb for the RIO GRANDE ZEPHYR as it comes gliding out of a mountain sunset to begin the long, spectacular descent to Denver. Rolling down at 40 miles per hour, and just passing

the west end of Tolland's 121 car siding, the 5771 leads the five car train on towards more high greens. On the high summer days of June and July it was generally daylight all the way for #18, and Denver will be a fascinating sight at twilight as the RGZ rolls out the tunnels and past Plainview. Elsewhere in passenger railroading, Amtrak is enduring its seemingly unending birth pangs, but here on July 16, 1972 the spirit of the CALIFORNIA ZEPHYR is still alive and well thanks to the railroad's decision not to accept the NRPC contract a year ago.

*(Above - Roland P. Parsons, below - Robert W. Andrews)*

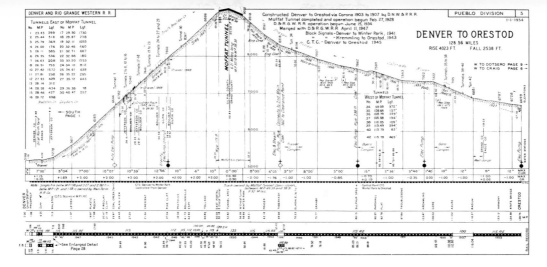

On June 11, 1953, when four-units were standard power for all freights, when nose plugs were something worn by swimmers, and before geeps were integrated into power consists, a one year old #5714 crossed South Boulder Creek while plodding resolutely west on the last few miles to East Portal. At that time tonnage ratings were computed on the basis of four unit sets, and only on rare occasions was any other combination used. The idea of any other combination was several years in the future, and even after the 1950 renumbering most F7s were operated sequentially numbered in four unit sets. Perhaps the early hassle over the FTs, the legal matters involved with "double header rules," and Brotherhood demands for additional crews on all cab units also had something to do with it, but in any case unit mixing was several years in the future.

The June 1952 order for seven 4 unit F7s, which were the Rio Grande's first units delivered in the orange and silver were notable on several counts. For they were the last F7s received by the line, were delivered at Lincoln, Nebraska on the Burlington to avoid Colorado sales tax, and arrived just in time to help move a traffic surge occasioned by the diversion of considerable Santa Fe and SP traffic to the central route after the Tehachpi earthquake put that rail route out of commission. Their arrival also made possible the dieselization of almost all non-peak period mainline freights, and enabled the shifting of the FTs to helper service. #5714 would also meet a kinder fate than the junkyards of La-Grange for it was one of those units sold for service on the Alaska Railroad.

*(Don Ball Collection)*

# East Portal

East Portal of the Moffat Tunnel
6.2 Mile Bore Through the Continental Divide

Most of us are familiar with the publicity pictures by the railroad of East Portal in the spring, with water gently bubbling from the tunnel which supplies Denver with so much of its drinking water, and James Peak shining in sunshine, while sightseers await the thrill of seeing a train pop from the bowels of the earth. Yes, it is all true, but there is another side. Cold, lonely, and snow covered, as in the following scenes all taken during those months when the fan operator and the sectionmen would be the only ones present to greet passing trains.

*(Below)* In the first, taken in February of 1962, THE YAMPA VALLEY MAIL awaits the eastbound passage of a freight led by #5574. It is a cold, frosty morning, and the morning sun has yet to cast its rays on the area of the tunnel.

*(Opposite page, top)* Just a year later, snow flakes are falling and #6013 slows for a flag stop after its 13 minute passage from Winter Park. Soon the Alco and its three car consist will be off in a swirl of snow and steam towards Denver, and the westbound freight on which the photographer was head brakeman will pull off the siding and thread its way west under the divide.

*(Opposite page, bottom)* In a variation on the earlier scene, F7 #5554 is in charge of #10 and is heading east bearing the marks of an encounter with a western slope snow drift. It is beginning to clear after the storm and the sun should be shining on the slopes an hour or so after the 1:35 PM passage.

*(Above - Wesley L. Haas, opposite page, both - Roland P. Parsons)*

# Winter Park

*(Above)* On a snowy February 5, 1959, Spreader #048 extends its wing to clear off the station platform before heading home. Tomorrow, the storm will have ended and the platform will stay cleared for the mob of ski train passengers which will descend on Winter Park. The storms of winter were such as to never require the use of rotaries, but Mr. Jordan's contraption came in most handy during the winter months for clearing out passing tracks, sidings, switches, and most anything else in Middle Park or elsewhere on the line. The climate in Colorado is such that quite often the roadmaster and his crew are engaged in activities like this at the same time their associates in the Traffic Department at Denver might be setting up a golf game there with a major shipper.

*(Opposite page)* The weather is a little bit different five years later on August 29, 1964, as #5604 leads the high cars of an SPD section east over the 2%. Fellow F7 #5731 is in charge of the Tabernash helpers today which will continue their exertions beyond to the apex of the tunnel where they will cut off and back down to their base. Even after attaining the 9,058 foot altitude here, there is still 3.9 miles of .9% before the tunnel apex is reached. Visible at the reader's right and just over the first freight cars are the scars on the hillside left by the D&SL's Rollins Pass line curving back and forth to gain altitude.

#5604 still has eight years of service before being traded in on a GP40-2, and #5731 while three years younger, will be stricken from the roster in the same year. While the second SPD today may not be typical of the "short, fast, frequent era" it is good example of the type of the freights run during many of the years described, with both sets in the 8th notch, and headed east with full tonnage.

*(Above - Vicktor Laszlow, opposite page, both - Ross B. Grenard)*

# Byers, Gore Canyon, and Orestod

After dropping down the hill to Tabernash, and passing through several short canyons, the railroad encounters the Colorado River which it will follow all the way into Utah, and crosses Middle Park, one of three such vast areas in Colorado's mountains wherein rise the two branches of the Platte and here, the Colorado. The first canyon in which the Colorado shares space with the Rio Grande is Byers, just west of Hot Sulphur Springs, and named for the pioneer Denver newspaper publisher William J. Byers, who had vast land holdings in this area.

Gore Canyon of the Colorado River
Moffat Tunnel Route

*(Opposite page, top)* While comparatively short and not as spectacular as Gore or Glenwood, Byers is quite attractive as proven in this portrait of an offpeak eight car CALIFORNIA ZEPHYR heading west in November of 1969. From here after negotiating the 15 degree curves of the Canyon, the track continues on through Parshall, Troublesome, and Kremmling. West of Kremmling there occurs something practically unheard of on the Rio Grande - three miles of absolutely level track with no grade in either direction!

*(Opposite page, bottom)* At the end of this phenomenon, Gore, finds the line heading into ten mile long Gore Canyon, whose depth is greater than the Royal Gorge and whose propensity to strike back at those who have dared to build and operate a railroad through its depths is legendary. Here on an April morning a westbound freight is shown in the depths about to traverse Tunnel #35 as it snakes its way toward Bond and Grand Junction. It was the decision by the D,NW&P to build through the canyon here that made possible the eventual link-up with the Rio Grande mainline for otherwise the cost of the Dotsero Cutoff would have been so great as to cause even the RFC, in the New Deal days, to have questioned its logic and cost-benefit ratio.

*(Above)* At Orestod, which as all good Rio Grande fans are aware, is Dotsero spelled backward, the Moffat Road took off up the side of the hill on its way west to the coal fields, Steamboat Springs and, it was dreamt, Utah. The D&SL only got to Craig, but Orestod is still the jumping off place for the Craig Branch. Just east of the division point of Bond, it was the often used for meets involving passenger trains, as here, in March 1970, where the CALIFORNIA ZEPHYR meets some eastbound tonnage behind #5328.

*(Opposite page, top - David Barret, opposite page, bottom - Ronald C. Hill, Grenard Collection, above - Roland P. Parsons)*

# Bond

Bond was established as a division point by reason of its being 131.5 miles from Denver and at the northern end of the 38 mile Dotsero Cutoff. In 1934, it was about the maximum distance that a freight crew could operate over the Moffat Tunnel Line without "outlawing" under the *Hours of Service Act* (D&SL crews could make it to Phippsburg but that is another story). It was also an engine change point during the years prior to 1939 when many of the Rio Grande's larger locomotives were precluded from operating on the D&SL trackage.

*(Below)* Since the Moffat Line took off at Orestod, its trains generally bypassed Bond continuing on the line which overlooked the community. In this scene, the last YAMPA VALLEY makes its passenger stop while the F9 hauling the ceremonial last run pauses in Bond. The date is Sunday April 7, as dictated by the Colorado PUC, so the excursion commemorating the end of passenger service operated over the weekend, leaving the final #9 to operate without fanfare.

*(Opposite page, top)* Missing its front coupler pocket as the result of an encounter with a boulder in Rock Creek Canyon the day before, #5771 stands at Bond with the ceremonial "last run" of #10. The crowd which showed up for this trip was so great that it required every passenger car the Rio Grande could scrape up, together with a couple of coaches borrowed from the UP, and several privately-owned cars as well. The result, shown here at Bond, required 4 units and had to be serviced at Bond on the return trip.

*(Opposite page, bottom)* Bond (population 150), like Salida and Minturn before it, was created by the Rio Grande as a division point. It had no other function in life and the systole and diastole of its existence were the trains which paused there to change crews. If one wished to eat or sleep, the railroad hotel was the only option. The company surgeon at Kremmling was the only doctor, and if other "creature comforts" were required a car ride to Glenwood, Eagle, or some other community was necessary.

Over the years of its existence, uncounted trains paused there, but none were so colorful, during the diesel era, as were the Burlington units operated in the relatively short-lived Chicago-Salt Lake pool described earlier. Here a quintet of Chinese red GP35s brightens up the scene in December 1965 as they await the highball on their eastward trek.

*(Below and opposite page, top - James Ozment, opposite page, bottom - Roland P. Parsons)*

# Dotsero Cutoff

The Dotsero Cutoff was the last major mainline to be constructed in Colorado, and was the last of the West's transcontinental linkups, establishing as it did a new route to the West Coast via Denver, something the Burlington had devoutly wished for ever since the 1880s. It was constructed by the Denver and Salt Lake Western, during the depths of the Depression, and financed by the Reconstruction Finance Corporation. Its legal and engineering history are beyond the scope of this volume, so suffice only to say that construction began in 1932 and was finished in 1934, that no previous railroad in Colorado had been built to as high a standard, and that it has justified its existence handsomely over the past half century.

Bond, at the northern end, functioned as we have seen as a division point and engine facility. Although the dieselization of the line eliminated this function, the engine house at Bond still had some customers in 1950, as the 3608 was fired up to handle an extra west. From the beginning the Rio Grande's largest power could be operated into Bond, but had to be changed out because of the light trestles, weak fills, and sharp curves which characterized the D&SL at that time. The steam facilities there were not retired until the late 1950s.

*(Don Ball Collection)*

| Mile Posts | Sub-Division 4-A STATIONS TIME-TABLE No. 132 OCT. 10, 1948 | | Miles from Dotsero |
|---|---|---|---|
| 128.6 | OD | ORESTOD JDN | 38.2 |
| | | 0.7 | |
| 129.3 | BX | BOND WFSYKBDN | 37.5 |
| | | 5.6 | |
| 134.9 | | GLEN | 31.9 |
| | | 7.2 | |
| 142.1 | | DELL | 24.7 |
| | | 2.5 | |
| 144.6 | | BURNS | 22.2 |
| | | 4.2 | |
| 148.8 | | SYLVAN | 18.0 |
| | | 6.5 | |
| 155.3 | | RANGE W | 11.5 |
| | | 2.4 | |
| 157.7 | | SWEETWATER | 9.1 |
| | | 5.5 | |
| 163.2 | | NICHE | 3.6 |
| | | 3.6 | |
| 166.8 | DY | DOTSERO JYDN | |
| | | (38.2) | |

Automatic Block Signals

Schedule Time
**Average** Speed per Hour

As a rule, action scenes on the thirty-eight miles from Bond south are rather hard to come by, if for no other reason than that it was so isolated from centers of population. Here, though, are two which do show what it was like in the days when the Rio Grande operated its own passenger trains.

*(Right)* In the first, #5761 and one of the two Alco PBs converted to steam generator cars get the westbound CALIFORNIA ZEPHYR out of town after stopping to change engine crews. With snow on the ground, and the Colorado River close beside it, the CZ begins its last year on a fine sunny day.

*(Left)* Alcos were still regular power on the "Silver Lady" in 1958, when #6003 headed through one of the cuts on July 10th. Commercial jets have yet to go into service, and the CZ still carries capacity crowds at almost all times. In this scene just north of Burns, the only community of any importance on the line, a little bit of the underlying geology is shown as #17 moves west through one of the cuts protected by a slide detector fence.

*(Above - Michael Davis, below - Vicktor Laszlow)*

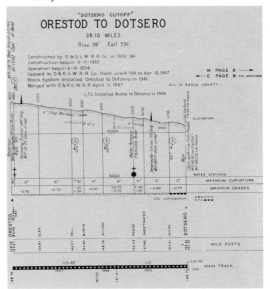

# Glenwood Canyon

The romance between the Rio Grande and the impassive and breathtaking topography of Glenwood Canyon commenced shortly after it began operation over the line and has continued ever since. Its great red shoulders have inspired uncounted tourists, motivated a General Motors VP to work out the concept of the *Vista Dome*, and been the background for innumerable publicity photos.

*(Opposite page)* In the first of these, here is the 1948 EXPOSITION FLYER, with many of the CZ coaches, buffet lounge, and diner already delivered, rounding a curve in the lower canon. A classic view, it appeared on Rio Grande timetables, ticket envelopes and in the annual report. It is an excellent example of how to accomplish one's goals without outright prevarication, for by posing #5 right here, only the new equipment showed and the standard weight Pullmans, open platform observation car et al were discreetly hidden from view.

*(Above)* The other, showing the westbound CALIFORNIA ZEPHYR behind PA 6001 and company, passing the "Monument To An Idea" at the spot where Cyrus Osborn, riding an FT cab, conceived the idea which brought a minor revolution to the passenger business. Taken on August 16, 1955, it graced the company's annual report, and a print of it once adorned many of the Rio Grande's offices.

Today Amtrak's CALIFORNIA ZEPHYR operates through a changed Canon, where construction on Interstate 70 brought about the removal of the car model and stone work. There are no domes on the train, and Cyrus Osburn's name is largely forgotten. The memorial has been placed at the Colorado Railroad Museum, and can be seen there, a reminder of a time not long ago when America's railroads regarded passengers as honored guests who were treated to both hospitality and innovation, particularly on railroads such as the Rio Grande.

*(Both - Otto Roach, D&RGW Collection, Denver Public Library, Western History Department)*

# Glenwood Springs

*(Below)* If the passengers regarded Glenwood Canyon as an experience and the railroad's headquarters as part of a romance which culminated during the 1940s and 50s, most railroaders concerned with the "nitty-gritty" of operating and maintaining a railroad through its 16.89 miles thought differently for reasons amply illustrated in this picture. Here, before the advent of high rail vehicles, a supervisor's motor car poses at Shoshone Tunnel in the heart of the canyon, on a sunny but cold January 25, 1962. Easily seen here are the slide fences, tunnel icicles, and so much of what is remembered by almost everyone familiar with railroad operation during the winter.

*(Opposite page, top)* Glenwood Springs has been a mecca for both the tourist and those seeking to take the waters. The development of Aspen in recent decades has added skiing to the menu, and the Rio Grande was only too happy to help carry them. So happy in fact, that on January 1, 1966 it got together with the CB&Q to operate an advance CALIFORNIA ZEPHYR from Glenwood to Chicago in order to take care of a massive overflow of business on the CZ. It utilized the spare observation-lounge constructed for the "Q" in 1952, all the lightweight cars that could be scraped up by both railroads, and some Espee sleepers. Assembled in Grand Junction it operated one way only behind GP30s and the steam generator car to Denver, where Burlington E-units took over. Here it is from the rear as it pulls out for parts east.

*(Opposite page, bottom)* A year later, both the sun and the SD45 demonstrators were out as the visitors from La Grange headed a freight train west. The rationale for their trip on February 17, 1967 would seem a little strange as the first Rio Grande units of this model were delivered a month earlier. In this scene at Chacra a few miles west, the 3600 horsepower units have a westbound manifest in tow, but neither the railroad's dynamometer or the EMD test car are present. *(All - Vicktor Laszlow)*

# West of Glenwood

*(Above)* Almost immediately after leaving the Glenwood Springs station, the mainline crossed the Colorado River to enter Funston Yard. Originally the originating point for Aspen Branch freights and the "Daily Excitement" which was at the end, the last of all standard gauge mixeds on the railroad, Funston also served as a helper station for eastbounds, a coal and water stop, CTC board, and countless other functions. It was abandoned shortly after this picture of the Rio Grande's last GP30 was snapped and relocated to make way for the Interstate Highway. The railroad was relocated to the opposite side of the Colorado River on an alignment once used by the long-gone Colorado Midland.

*(Opposite page, top)* The construction on the Glenwood line change began in early 1967, and was very much "state of the art" for 1966. Its construction methods featured helicopters and heavy machinery never envisioned by the forces of the CM and D&RG which raced each other to see who could get down the Grand Valley to Grand Junction first. It was one of the first truly modern, computerized line changes undertaken by the Rio Grande. Here the eastbound CALIFORNIA ZEPHYR rolls by while construction and grading proceed on what had been the Midland side of the river.

*(Opposite page, bottom)* While the Glenwood line change was an accomplishment and no doubt many derived great satisfaction from riding domes over former Colorado Midland right-of-way, it did deprive photographers of some excellent photo locations as here, of the CALIFORNIA ZEPHYR leaving Funston. The track is straighter, and the bridge which curved so eloquently into Glenwood Springs is gone, but for those who liked the old line there is little to do. In this June 19, 1966 scene, #5771 has an eleven car train rolling west and will soon reach Rifle Creek, where once the Rio Grande and Colorado Midland began shared track into Grand Junction.

*(All - Vicktor Laszlow)*

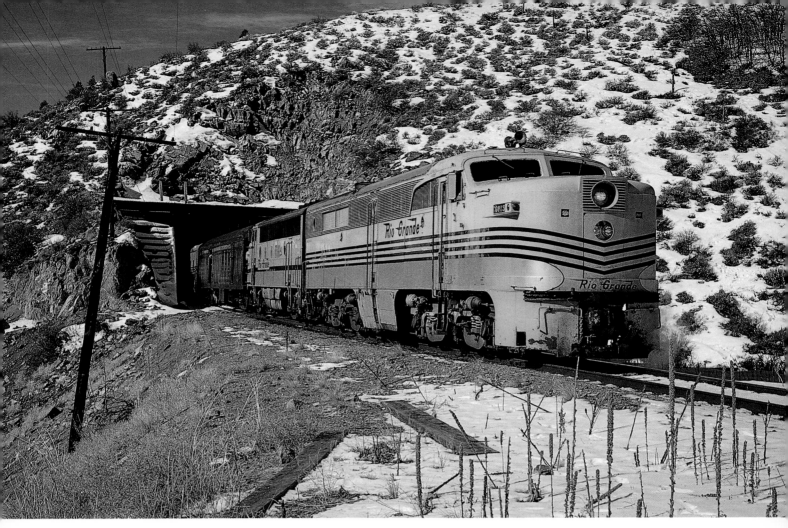

# Craig Branch

That part of the Rio Grande stretching west from Orestod to Craig is one of bittersweet memories, for it was intended to be a transcontinental mainline, and in the 1920s was almost completed to Salt Lake City, something which remains one of the great "Might Have Beens" in Colorado railroad history. After the completion of the Moffat Tunnel, Utah interests headed by traction magnates Julian and Simon Bamberger were interested in completing the line from its end point at Craig, Colorado. The Dotsero Cutoff ended that and the dream of David Moffat for all time and it remains, even today, the Craig Branch. On the other hand, the D&SL, and its corporate successors have profited greatly from the business generated on the line, chiefly coal, which in the late 1970s justified CTC and welded rail to Phippsburg. The Rangely oil field, a Texaco refinery at Craig, wheat, livestock, and lumber have all contributed over the years, and it still remains a viable part of Mr. Anschutz's railroad.

*(Opposite page, top)* It is a mountain railroad in the finest sense of the word, and not every trip over it went as intended. Here, near Volcano, an SD45 confronts a rockslide while leading an eastbound coal train.

*(Opposite page, bottom)* Such rockslides were no respecters of passenger trains, as here in February of 1965, when one of the Intermountain Chapter NRHS's several "last runs" came to grief at a tunnel in Rock Creek Canyon. Such rockslides were generally the railroad equivalent of "fender benders" but could and did cause injury and damage. Over the years, the Rio Grande has applied layer upon layer of technology to its plant in a largely successful effort to avoid such problems, and a standard caveat contained in every train order issued from fall to late spring reads *LOOK OUT FOR ROCKS WHERE LIABLE TO FALL."*

*(Above)* Things were a little brighter on the trip the year before, as the ubiquitous #6013 led Train #10 out of Tunnel #53 in Egeria Canyon. The 129 foot bore was essentially as built in 1910, and had seen the passage of uncounted trains carrying coal, oil, wheat, livestock and travelers from throughout the world who compared the eastward slope of the Toponas Divide to the mountain railroads of Switzerland or to the finest scenery the narrow gauge had to offer.

*(Opposite page, top - David Barret, opposite page, bottom - Henry Bender, Grenard Collection, above - Ross B. Grenard)*

# Along the Craig Branch

*(Opposite page, top)* Lying some 168 miles west of Denver, Phippsburg was the division point and marshaling yard for traffic off the west end. Named for Lawrence C. Phipps, late U.S. Senator from Colorado and one of those who by their investment and faith in his railroad helped keep David Moffat's dream alive, it was cold in the winter, rather bleak much of the time, and substantially underlaid with coal. It is here that eastbound unit trains are assembled for their journeys to power plants, and units added for the grades which lie ahead. In a snowy scene a few years ago at the servicing facility, GP30 #3004 and "Tunnel Motor" #5356 idled away an afternoon.

| Mile Posts | | STATIONS | | Miles from Craig |
|---|---|---|---|---|
| | | **CRAIG BRANCH** | | |
| | | Sub-Division 1-B | | |
| | | STATIONS | | |
| | | TIME-TABLE No. 1 | | |
| | | APRIL 16, 1961 | | |
| 168.0 | BG | **PHIPPSBURG** | DNBFKO SWY | 63.7 |
| | | 3.4 | | |
| 171.4 | | OAK CREEK | | 60.3 |
| | | 2.2 | | |
| 173.6 | | ROUTT | | 58.1 |
| | | 1.6 | | |
| 175.2 | | HAYBRO | | 56.5 |
| | | 3.0 | | |
| 178.2 | | PARK | | 53.5 |
| | | 5.7 | | |
| 183.9 | | SIDNEY | | 47.8 |
| | | 7.2 | | |
| 191.1 | 8 | STEAMBOAT | D | 40.6 |
| | | 10.1 | | |
| 201.2 | | MILNER | | 30.5 |
| | | 5.4 | | |
| 206.6 | | BEAR | | 25.1 |
| | | 1.4 | | |
| 208.0 | | HARRIS | | 23.7 |
| | | 7.1 | | |
| 215.1 | HN | HAYDEN | D | 16.6 |
| | | 16.6 | | |
| 231.7 | CG | **CRAIG** | DBFKWY | 0.0 |

*(Opposite page, bottom)* At Steamboat Springs, the railroad enters the lush and verdant valley of the Yampa River. Here on a pleasant September 24, 1959, the area's namesake train pauses at the station before continuing on its eastward journey. The paucity of business indicates why Stout Street is already making noises about discontinuing the train. To these, local residents counter that they are subsidizing its operation through their taxes to the Moffat Tunnel Improvement District (the entity which floated the bonds to build the tunnel) and are prepared to jam them down the ICC's throat if the railroad would care to try and exert its powers under the *Transportation Act of 1958*. Stay tuned by all means, as a veritable soap opera ensues.

*(Above)* On June 25, 1959, Train #9 approaches Tunnel #55, 404' long and the last one on the way to Craig. #6001 leads the two car train up the final major hill before starting downgrade to its namesake valley. Trodding in the footsteps of 4-6-0s, 2-8-0s, Mallets, and Rio Grande steam engines including the mighty 3600s, the Alco PA and its two car train created a classic of the early diesel era here.

*(Opposite page, top - Ronald C. Hill, Grenard Collection, opposite page, bottom and above - Vicktor Laszlow)*

# Craig

*(Above)* With two cars and #6013 providing the power, Train #10 looks into the morning sun as it prepares to head east with only a baggage car and one of the 1000 series coaches rebuilt for EXPOSITION FLYER service in the consist. In later days, 9 and 10 will add and then subtract an RPO car, carry dome cars, and privately owned equipment in its consist until the fate of all good passenger trains overtakes it. One may, indeed wonder what the D&SL veterans who manned the trains during its early days and have since passed on would say if they were to return and discover that the source of their livelihood had, in the end, acquired a national reputation as one of the ultimate train rides in America.

*(Opposite page, top)* After the RS3s originally purchased to dieselize the Craig Branch were removed to other assignments, SDs became the power of choice for mine runs, locals, and other capacities. Here #5311, still in its EMD applied paint job, almost a decade after leaving LaGrange, poses beside the wool loading shed at Craig. After the crew's rest it will head back to Phippsburg amid the snows of December 1966.

*(Opposite page, bottom)* In another perspective, #5311 strikes the "beauty and the beast" pose with PA #6001, which has made it into the new single stripe image. In a few minutes, the YAMPA VALLEY (so named after the mail contract was lost) will back into the Craig Station to begin its loading process. Having dodged the bullet of discontinuance for the last few years, #10 is about to lose the PAs which have been so much a part of its mystique since it was reincarnated in Sept. 1954.

*(Above - Vicktor Laszlow, opposite page, both - James B. Calvert)*

| Table 5 | | | DENVER, WINTER PARK, GRANBY, STEAMBOAT SPRINGS AND CRAIG | | | |
|---|---|---|---|---|---|---|
| **READ DOWN** | | Miles | STATIONS | Eleva-tion | **READ UP** | |
| No. 23 | No. 9 | | | | No. 10 | No. 24 |
| c 8 20 pm | * 9 25 am | 0 | Lv Denver.........Ar | 5280 | * 3 15 pm | 6 20 am |
| f 8 38 " | f 9 38 " | 4 | Lv Zuni............Lv | 5211 | f 3 02 " | ........ |
| | f 9 43 " | 7 | Lv Ralston.........Lv | 5258 | f 2 57 " | ........ |
| | f 9 53 " | 12 | Lv Leyden Junction.Lv | 5617 | f 2 47 " | ........ |
| f 9 35 pm | f10 23 " | 24 | Lv Plainview.......Lv | 6782 | f 2 15 " | 4 55 am |
| | f10 45 " | 31 | Lv Crescent........Lv | 7441 | f 1 53 " | ........ |
| 10 19 pm | 11 05 " | 37 | Lv Pine Cliff.......Lv | 7966 | 1 33 " | 4 12 am |
| 10 33 " | 11 18 " | 42 | Lv Rollinsville......Lv | 8367 | 1 18 " | 3 57 " |
| f10 48 " | f11 30 " | 47 | Lv Tolland.........Lv | 8886 | f 1 06 " | f 3 45 " |
| 10 56 " | 11 37 " | 50 | Lv East Portal.....Lv (Moffat Tunnel) | 9197 | 1 00 " | 3 35 " |
| 11 16 pm | 11 52 am | 57 | Lv Winter Park.....Lv | 9076 | 12 42 pm | 3 15 am |
| 11 32 " | 12 04 pm | 62 | Lv Fraser..........Lv | 8561 | 12 24 " | 2 50 " |
| 11 40 " | 12 12 " | 66 | Lv Tabernash.......Lv | 8318 | 12 12 " | 2 40 " |
| | f12 17 " | 70 | Lv Elkdale.........Lv | 8156 | f11 55 am | ........ |
| 12 06 am | 12 35 " | 76 | Lv Granby.........Lv | 7937 | 11 50 " | 2 10 am |
| | f12 40 " | 80 | Lv Drowsy Water...Lv | 7790 | f11 37 " | ........ |
| 12 30 am | 12 50 " | 86 | LvHotSulphurSpgs..Lv | 7662 | 11 30 " | 1 35 am |
| f12 51 " | f12 55 " | 91 | Lv Parshall........Lv | 7589 | f11 20 " | f 1 15 " |
| 1 21 " | 1 19 " | 103 | Lv Kremmling......Lv | 7322 | 11 03 " | 12 55 " |
| | f 1 23 " | 106 | Lv Gore...........Lv | 7322 | f10 55 " | ........ |
| 2 00 am | 1 48 " | 117 | Lv Radium.........Lv | 6858 | 10 31 " | f12 20 am |
| 2 18 " | f 2 03 " | 126 | Lv State Bridge.....Lv | 6728 | f10 13 " | f11 57 pm |
| 2 35 " | 2 13 " | 129 | Lv **Orestod**........Lv | 6710 | 10 10 " | 11 50 " |
| 2 53 " | 2 30 " | 134 | Lv McCoy.........Lv | 7228 | 9 52 " | f11 20 " |
| | f 2 53 " | 143 | Lv Volcano........Lv | 7807 | f 9 30 " | ........ |
| | f 3 13 " | 150 | Lv Egeria.........Lv | 8123 | f 9 11 " | ........ |
| f 3 51 am | 3 18 " | 153 | Lv Toponas........Lv | 8264 | 9 06 " | f10 23 pm |
| 4 13 " | 3 35 " | 162 | Lv Yampa.........Lv | 7882 | 8 52 " | 10 00 " |
| 4 45 " | 4 00 " | 168 | Lv Phippsburg.....Lv | 7413 | 8 40 " | 9 35 " |
| 5 05 " | 4 10 " | 171 | Lv Oak Creek......Lv | 7397 | 8 15 " | 9 18 " |
| f 5 07 " | f 4 12 " | 172 | Lv Oak Hills.......Lv | 7372 | f 8 13 " | f 9 17 " |
| 5 16 " | 4 19 " | 175 | Lv Haybro.........Lv | 7169 | 8 06 " | f 9 10 " |
| f 5 30 " | f 4 36 " | 184 | Lv Sidney.........Lv | 6823 | f 7 53 " | f 8 53 " |
| 6 01 " | 4 57 " | 191 | Lv **Steamboat Spgs.**.Lv | 6682 | 7 42 " | 8 40 " |
| f 6 11 " | f 5 08 " | 198 | Lv Brookston......Lv | 6529 | f 7 26 " | f 8 18 " |
| 6 19 " | 5 14 " | 201 | Lv Milner.........Lv | 6480 | 7 21 " | f 8 12 " |
| f 6 29 " | f 5 22 " | 206 | Lv Bear River......Lv | 6425 | f 7 13 " | f 8 02 " |
| 6 38 " | 5 29 " | 208 | Lv Mt. Harris......Lv | 6413 | 7 10 " | 7 58 " |
| 6 58 " | 5 45 " | 215 | Lv **Hayden**.........Lv | 6328 | 6 58 " | 7 43 " |
| f 7 10 " | f 5 51 " | 219 | Lv Cary Ranch.....Lv | 6278 | f 6 49 " | f 7 34 " |
| 7 45 " | 6 35 " | 231 | Ar **Craig**..........Lv | 6174 | * 6 30 " | k 7 15 " |

# Aspen Branch

Dating back to 1887, the branch to Aspen was built to serve the immense mineral riches of the area, which were then sufficient to justify at least in part, the construction of the Tennessee Pass line on what was termed "The Aspen Extension." Aspen also figured heavily in the plans to construct the Colorado Midland, so great was its traffic potential. This story, although interesting, has been covered extensively in both Morris Cafky's *Colorado Midland* and Robert Athearn's *Rebel Of The Rockies*, and the reader is referred to them for the detailed history. The 1893 "silver crash" ended Aspen's boom days but it has achieved prominence in recent years as a ski resort and a community of the wealthy on a scale never imagined by the good general when he founded Colorado Springs to be "the Newport of the Rockies." The Rio Grande, as a survivor, continued to service what business remained here with the "Daily Excitement," a rather reclusive standard gauge mixed which lasted until 1948 and seasonal extras to serve the livestock, potato, and coal business from Carbondale and Cattle Creek.

| Mile Posts | | Sub-Division 4-B STATIONS TIME-TABLE No. 1 APRIL 16, 1961 | | Miles from Aspen |
|---|---|---|---|---|
| 360.1 | GN | GLENWOOD | P | 41.2 |
| 367.9 | | CATTLE CREEK | | 33.4 |
| 373.0 | | CARBONDALE | D | 28.3 |
| 379.4 | | LEON | | 21.9 |
| 382.0 | | EMMA | | 19.3 |
| 392.9 | | WOODY CREEK | | 8.4 |
| 401.3 | | ASPEN | Y | |

*(Above)* For some strange reason, very few pictures were taken on the branch during steam days, so we have little to remind us of the ten-wheelers and 2-8-0s which were the principal power on the line, but here is #5904 leading a string of coal empties up the Roaring Fork Valley on their way for loading at Kaiser Steel's mine near Carbondale. The valley had been noted for the high quality of its metallurgical coal for many years and this was a strong motivation for both the CM and the D&RG to expand into the area.

*(Left)* Six months after the December 7, 1966 scene, SD7 #5308 was in charge of the coal train as it headed south near Cattle Creek. By this time, the branch had been largely cut back to Woody Creek, some 8.4 miles from Aspen, where ore deposits constituted the only business south of Mid Continent's coal mine.

*(Both - Vicktor Laszlow)*

*(Right)* On April 12, 1959, the eminent Colorado railroad historian Bob Richardson, made a trip to the Roaring Fork Valley, and here is shown (at left) with one of his associates inspecting the D&RG depot at Aspen, where once overnight pullmans loaded passengers and cars of silver ore were billed. No longer even meriting the services of an agent, it was then being occupied as a home and the probability of it ever becoming again a rail center were nearly nil.

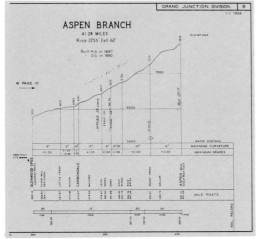

*(Below)* While the snows of winter have been a heaven-sent miracle to the citizens of Aspen whose prosperity is in large part based on its popularity as a winter sports center, it was a mixed blessing to those responsible for maintaining railroad service. Here, at Woody Creek on March 13, 1962, the roadmaster contemplates his spreader plow which is now off the track and in the ditch. GP7 #5108 idles in the background, as decisions of major import are under consideration.
*(Both - Vicktor Laszlow)*

# L'envoi

East of Grand Junction, on November 2, 1968, rolls Denver-bound freight #154, headed by #5317 and a trio of SD45s. Traveling over what was once the jointly-operated Rio Grande Junction which is forever populated with the ghosts of the long-departed Colorado Midland, the 10,800 horsepower consist is powering a train of such tonnage and at such a speed as to make the railroaders of that early day shake their heads in disbelief. And yet this too is but a memory today in the railroad's long, stormy past, and recent triumphs.

For the Rio Grande has been in its time, both ever changing and eternally fascinating, qualities that have endeared it to many and account for its ability to capture the imagination. It is these qualities we hope to have shown you in this volume, and which we plan to show in a later work covering a different Rio Grande as it makes its way west across the desert and mountains of Utah, and through an area of weirdly eroded sandstones to a terminus beside a great inland sea. *(Mike Davis)*